POLICY

OF

MANIPULATION

A PERSONAL HISTORY OF OGUN STATE

....

BY

ZENTS KUNLE SOWUNMI

(ORACLEZENTS)

KORLOKI PUBLISHERS INC

NEW YORK USA

2013

BEFORE

AND

AFTER

1976

What People Are Saying Zents

A provocative and elegant, complex and interesting political history I am glad this objective piece is from an Egba man

Prof Bankole Okuwa.
North Carolina USA

Sowunmi has successfully given us the hidden stories behind Ogun State problems. **Engr. Awolana**
General Manager OGBC Abeokuta

A provocative and thought revealing book on Ogun State politics
Ayinde Soaga
General Manager OGTV Abeokuta

Amazing revelation, with credibility from a writer who lived the dreams of the State

Chief Dauda Sokeye. Bronx New York USA

This Oracle is a credible source of our historical revelations
Paul Adujie. Port Harcourt. Nigeria

POLICY OF MANIPULATION

(A PERSONAL HISTORY OF OGUN STATE POLITICS)

BY

ZENTS K. SOWUNMI

ORACLEZENTS

For additional copies of this or other Zents Sowunmi titles write:

Korloki Publishers Inc.

P.O. Box 300605, Brooklyn, New York 11230

Please allow 4 to 6 weeks for delivery.

For bulk orders contact us via email

korlokipublishers@gmail.com

Copyright © 2013 by Zents Kunle Sowunmi
OGUN STATE: POLICY OF MANIPULATION SINCE 1976

Request for information should be addressed to Korloki Publishing Company P.O. Box 300605 Brooklyn NY 11230 USA

All rights reserved. Printed in the United States of America. No part of the author's original material may be reproduced, stored in a retrieval system or transmitted in any form or by any means –electronics, mechanical, photocopy, recording or any other–except for brief quotation in printed review, without the prior permission of the publisher.

Library of Congress Cataloging–in-publication Data

Cover design by: Sel P Graphic Designs.

Interior design: Korloki Publishers Inc., Brooklyn New York. USA
Photographs: Map of Ogun State/Nigeria /Africa/ Zents K Sowunmi/ Ojude festival/Habeeb Fawora/supplied online.

Summary: *The political and economic history of Ogun State from the suspended intra ethnic wars and words of pre-colonization before 1865 and political problems since 1976, the future, growth and challenges ahead.*

ISBN: 13 - 978-1936-739-24-0   ISBN: 10 – 19370739240

PRINTED IN USA

DEDICATION

This book is dedicated

To

Late **Oba Oyebade Mofolunso Lipede**

The Alake of Egbaland for his positive contributions to Egbaland 1972-2005

Ω

Governor Ibikunle Amosun

The first Ogun State Polytechnic Student to become the Governor of Ogun State

Ω

Late Sola Alakija and Kehinde Sokeye

Both were members of Ogun State Polytechnic Students Union and National union in 1980 with the Oracl

CONTENTS

Dedication 6

Appreciation 11

Foreword 15

Introduction 47

Chapter One — Behind the Mask 51

Chapter Two — Activities 69

Chapter Three — Minority Report 111

Chapter Four — New Leadership 131

Chapter Five — Dissolved Board of GPC 171

Chapter Six — Within 177

Chapter Seven — Next Step 185

Chapter Eight — Imaginations 191

Chapter Nine — The Ripples of Hope 207

Chapter Ten — The task ahead 213

Chapter Eleven — Two States Option 227

Chapter Twelve — Better Days ahead 235

OGUN STATE POLICY OF MANIPULATION SINCE 1976

(A PERSONAL HISTORY OF OGUN STATE POLITICS)

Other Books by Zents Kunle Sowunmi

- ❖ President Obama: Hero or villain of Capitalism?
- ❖ Before the Journey Became Home
- ❖ 100 ways to Laugh
- ❖ Cien Maneras de Reir
- ❖ What happened to Our Democracy?
- ❖ Not a stranger anymore
- ❖ Covenant Breakers
- ❖ Unequally Yoking
- ❖ The Vultures and Vulnerable

Coming soon!!

- ❖ The Loopholes
- ❖ The Price of Arab Revolution
- ❖ A Mischievous widow

Order copies of this author's books directly from

www.kpcbooks.com

KORLOKI PUBLISHERS Inc.

NEW YORK,

USA

APPRECIATION

Human being could be funny, when someone does you a favor, it is normal to say thank you, if you don't, it could be seen as being unreasonably ungrateful, and if you follow the tradition to say thank you, then you get another form of funny compliment, don't mention it, they will say.

Ogun State policy of manipulation since 1976 the book in your hand could never have been written or existed either as online article or as this present book in your hand without the encouragement of my readers on social media like Facebook, and as you read this book, note your contribution to the development of Ogun State just begun and I have no doubt you will do great things yourself on how to be a positive contributor to Ogun State.

I will like to show my appreciation to my online readers most of them I never met, like Olusesan Ekisola, Ogunyemi Dayo, Toye Asaju, Isquil Najim, Adebisi Osoba, Akinbode, Dr. Michael Adeyemi, Prof. Ramon, and Tunde Ilori when this book first came out as series of my articles which was my little contributions to the challenges faced by the people of Ogun State, as a result of that, I felt like digging more into how the problems started from what could have been the joy of the two old provinces of Ijebu and Egba in a new State but turned out to be different.

This book will reveal the good and the ugly side of Ogun State politics to the point of disgust, sometimes, with a naked display of ignorance; it will explain those factors dragging the State behind from catching up with the development in Lagos State or its inability to meet the challenges of being the economic hub of Nigeria in the 21st century.

This present publication has significantly profited from conversations, and reading of numbers of journal, articles, monitoring of events and researches which enriched my understanding of Ogun State politics.

I will like to appreciate the honest and past support of the following people to my academic chases, and social development, late Bishop Finn and Bishop Alaba Job and Father Clifford of Catholic dioceses at Ibadan in the sixties, and the following teachers, late Akindele and Agunbiade of St Paul Primary school in 1969 and Mr. Oyewole known to us his students at Lisabi Grammar School in the early seventies as *"Baba Wolimoh"* which was his ways of indicating to us, he was going to be tough on us.

Also for the support of Justice Deinde Soremi, my cousins, Adejare Shoyoye, and Adebayo Shoyoye, the staff of National Achieves Ibadan in my formative years, and the workers of University of Ibadan like Professors Fafunso (late), Soyode, Doyin Soyibo, Patrick Oribabor, Jimi Adesina, and Hon. Sam Mazi Ohambuwa a onetime Sales Director for Pfizer Product Lagos.

My appreciation is also extended to Ms. Rainey Smith, who proof read the manuscript, Dr. Titilayo Onagoruwa and those who read the articles for their questions that eventually expanded this book, particularly one Akinbode who asked me to convert the articles to a book for posterity.

However, the book is written in a very simple way to make it easier for anyone with interest in Ogun State politics to understand and appreciate the efforts of the founding fathers of the State and goals ahead.

Furthermore, the objective of this book is to build not to destroy the efforts of past leaderships of the State since 1976 more importantly, to open up avenues for discussions on opportunities on how the State can utilize its diversity for prosperity.

All the facts as analyzed here, are purely my observations and experiences for academic purposes only, it could be emotional or sometimes full of humors as an Egba man, who lived the dreams of the new State from inception in 1976 and participated in most of the events in the State with various government agencies within and outside the Ogun State

I hope you will have value for your time or money if you actually bought a copy for reading this personal contribution to the political history of Ogun State because some of the stories might sound funny or ignorant by the actors, however, all facts mentioned here have not been embellished, because they actually occurred and I do accept obligation for all the facts of this book.

Again, please note this book is for critical thinking only on how to move the State forward not to tear it down, please don't expect more than this, it could be controversial even if you do not accepts my thesis, this is only a serious injection into serious political problems of Ogun State.

Finally, I will like to thank my children, Bidemi, her husband Femi Imoru and my son Peter Sowunmi all in Texas for giving me the space to write this book.

Zents Kunle Sowunmi
April 20, 2013

FOREWORD

By

Olusesan Ekisola

Rogers, Minnesota USA

For the sake of complete transparency, I want to begin this exercise by admitting upfront that I am a very proud son of Ogun State, and a particularly proud 'son of Ijebu soil' having been born to Ijebu parents from Imupa Quarters in Ijebu-Ode.

Now having thus disclosed my lineage, I also want to express my total admiration for the writer, whom I met online, on Facebook, to be precise, through his many writings. I was attracted to his precise and highly drilled-down comments on issues that attract his attention, no matter what these are: American politics, Nigeria wide subject-matters etc.

A very clear pointer to the eventuality of this great book, **Ogun State: Policy of Manipulation Since 1976**. He is frank and does not mince words expressing his views no matter whose goat he gets in the process. Hence my interest in recruiting him to write for an online publication I work on, African Outlook Online. And he never disappointed.

He sent in his write-ups like clockwork addressing issues of the day and matters of interest to Nigerians and Africans. He never shies away from controversial topics and handles them in a way that is inclusive and offer constructive engagement. In the course of this friendship, I observed that he is a well-respected commentator especially among his friends and followers on Facebook and an online Blog he authors.

So I developed more interest in his writings and when he asked me to take a look as this book: ***Ogun State – Policy of Manipulation Since 1976,*** I eagerly awaited the advance copy he promised. By the time I got it and another book on his personal life experience, I found out I could not put it down until I finished reading the whole thing in the course of a day and a half! I want to say here that the book is very interesting, well-written and chock-full of information on the State known as the Gateway State.

A Gateway, we are always reminded, to all that is good, and I dare add, (... bad!) about Nigeria! Ogun State has produced many of Nigeria's leaders in every field of endeavor known to man from politics to the professions and all engagements in-between.

An attempt to name names would be an impossible task to begin with but I must make the attempt even if I already know I will end up failing most woefully as I must because the State has produced so many eminent individuals that have played prominent roles in the history of our nation, Nigeria.

But I love the idea of this book because it has helped to add value to the State and its people by providing additional information on the early stage of its formation and the prevailing environment at the time from the writer's perspective.

This is a good step in the right direction because it should encourage others to also come forward with their verifiable experiences and world view of our great State. This is why I believe the book is a very important resource for all Ogun State citizens and their close relatives in neighboring States for we are all interwoven through marital linkages and other ties that bind us together.

The book reminds me of those good old days of early Ogun State and the shape of things in Abeokuta. It also reminds me of the relationships between all the groups that make up the new State. I am aware that Ijebus and Egbas have always been very close and friendly especially outside the State. Among the many observations

I have read and re-read this piece by Zents Sowunmi is my admiration for his candor in addressing the issue which most people would have left unremarked while clearly ignoring the elephant in the room.

The Egbas and Ijebus along with the other citizens of Ogun State, the Yewas and Aworis, and the many communities that make up the State, have a big stake in addressing what could be a ticking time bomb if it really exists or otherwise devote their energies to building a truly great State in every sense of the word.

Olusesan Ekisola

Rogers, Minnesota USA

2013

POLICY

OF

MANIPULATION

(A PERSONAL HISTORY OF OGUN STATE POLITICS)

BY

ZENTS K. SOWUNMI

An Overview of the City of Abeokuta from Olumo Rock

HRM Oba Adedotun Gbadebo

Alake of Egbaland since 2005

HRM Oba Oyebade Lipede

Late Alake of Egbaland 1972-2005

HRH Oba Sikiru Adetona

Awujale of Ijebuland since 1964

HRM Oba Kehinde Olugbenle
Olu of Ilaro Paramount ruler of Yewa Land

HRM Oba Adeniyi Sonariwo

Akarigbo of Remoland

Late Chief Obafemi Awolowo

He was like the re-incarnation of Oduduwa to the Yoruba

LATE GEN. MURITALA MOHAMMED

Military head State who created Ogun State in 1976

GEN. OLUSEGUN OBASANJO

Chief of Staff Supreme Headquarters, he became Head of State in 1976 after the assassination of Gen Muritala Mohamed

COL. AYODELE SEIDU BALOGUN

First Military Governor of Ogun State March 1976 - July 1978

BRIGADIER HARRIS EGHAGHA

Military Administrator July 1978-Oct. 1979

Late Chief Victor Bisi Onabanjo

(Ayekooto)

First Civilian Governor of Ogun State Oct. 1979 - Dec. 1983

BRIGADIER DIPO DIYA

Military Governor Jan. 1984-August 1985

BRIGADIER DAYO POPOOLA
Military Governor August 1985-1986

Brigadier Raji Alagbe Rasaki

Military Governor August 1986 – Dec 1987

Navy Captain Mohamed Lawal

Military Governor Dec 1987-Aug 1990

Rear Admiral Oladeinde Joseph

August 1990-Jan.1992

Chief Segun Osoba

Civilian Governor Jan. 1992-Nov. 1993

Col. Daniel Akintonde

Military Administrator Nov.1993 - August 1996

Group Captain Sam Ewang

Military Administrator In office   Aug. 1996 – Aug.1998

Navy Captain Kayode Olofin Moyin

Military Administrator In office   Aug. 1998 –May 1999

Chief Olusegun Osoba

Civilian Governor 1999-2003

Chief Otunba Gbenga Daniel

Civilian Governor May 2003 - May 2011

Senator Ibikunle Amosun

Civilian Governor May 2011 to date

Politics is the art of looking for trouble, finding it whether it exists or not, diagnosing it incorrectly, and applying the wrong remedy.

~Ernest Benn

INTRODUCTION

A Yoruba adage says, if you run into a lame man or cripple with a crooked load on his head early in the morning, you need not ask him why his load is crooked, all you need to do is to look at shape of his legs, the story here is for the future of Ogun State indigenes, indeed Nigerians, which our children and grandchildren will feel significantly energized to know the political formation of Ogun State in its simplest form on how it all started on February 3rd 1976, the year was significantly, an improvement in the lives of all Nigerians.

It marked the change of polices of the giant of Africa into a purposeful leadership. It witnessed the creation of more States from twelve to nineteen. It was a political decision which was in favor of the North of Nigeria in spite of its assumed limited population by the people of lower Niger.

However, within the South West of Nigeria itself, particularly among the Yoruba, intra-ethnic manipulation often led to frustrations on the goals towards an egalitarian society, among the new States, Ogun State represented the most detailed platform for the problems of intra-ethnic wars that were suspended when the British colonized Nigeria. It marked the beginning of a new war strategy, not physical but mental war on its people which will be the focus of this book.

This is a fearless personal history of Ogun State from 1976 to date, it is also a proper revelation of everything; this writer is often referred to, as "Oracle" on the social media because of his ability to predict events, he placed everything on the table, the good, the bad, and ugly of everything you have to know about the Gateway State of Nigeria.

Historically, Egba nation could be noted to be the first set of people within the Yoruba nation to introduce tolls on any route in 1865 on the traders using the Ikorodu route as the gateway to what eventually became Nigeria, before the British Army led by Glover, the Lieutenant General of the new Lagos Colony removed it, and by 1892 the Ijebu Army was also defeated by the British on what became the final stage or end of Yoruba wars.

The disagreement between the Egba nation and Ijebu was purely economic on who could control the slave and post-slave route to Lagos and Badagry and later over ammunition and salt core of the war between the them and other Yoruba.

The people of Ogun State by extension which was part of Western State could be found in major cities like Epe Ikorodu, Somolu on the Ijebu side and Abule Egba up to Agege, Ikeja, Mushin and Oyingbo, Badagry in Lagos State not as settlers, but as original owners of the Cities lost to the new Lagos State created on May 27, 1967 by the Military Government of General Yakubu Gowon.

In other words, almost forty percent of those in present day Lagos State could be classified as originally from what is now known as Ogun State, particularly, Egba and Ijebu provinces, and the administrative measurement tape of the British colonial system between 1860-1960.

However, don't be surprised that the great names you have appreciated and met in Lagos State like Williams, Willoughby, Tinubu, Bakare were probably from the present day Ogun State.

Ogun "Straight" or State was the way the people with arrested education pronounced the name of the State from both sides of the provinces due to the tick Yoruba ascent. It was funny in those days, and it marked the end of loyalty to Ibadan politics, now, it would be time for them to focus on developing their heritage.

Zents Kunle Sowunmi

"Honor is on its objective side, other people's opinion of what we are worth; on its subjective side, it is the respect we pay to this opinion." (Position, 1851)

Arthur Schopenhauer

7

BEHIND THE MASK

The creation of Ogun State out of the old Western State in Nigeria and the City of Abeokuta as the capital of the new State on February 3, 1976 was announced on Nigerian radios and televisions by General Muritala Mohammed, Nigeria Head of State.

At first, the announcement brought joy and smiles to the faces of the people, to them, it was assumed to be a surprise package left behind by the second in command, General Olusegun Aremu Obasanjo, the Chief of Staff Supreme Head Quarters.

The contention then was that the new Ogun State was manipulated to favor his people, the Egba, a sub-ethnic group among the Yoruba tribe south of the Sahara, and General Obasanjo's position of authority then was more like that of a Vice President, but the military had a different way to classify position of authority in those days, he was the administrative brain behind the Federal Military Government of Nigeria as Chief of Staff Supreme Head Quarters.

The announcement of the creation of the new seven States came at a time General Olusegun Obasanjo was on his way, on behalf of the Federal Republic of Nigeria to attend the MPLA meeting with the rebel leader Augustinho Neto in Angola who later in life became the country's first post-independence President.

However, Neto's new socialist party which the Nigerian government supported toward the independence of Angola won on the long run. It was the best foreign policy in Nigeria since 1960.

The support of Nigeria for Augustinho Neto, however, created bad blood between the government of Nigeria and the United States of America, under the Presidency of the late Gerald Ford who wanted a Savinbi led pro-capitalist group that was sympathetic to western interests as the president of the yet to be freed country from the years of colonization.

The United States America's government and her people hated anything that smells or thinks like socialism unfortunately, the Soviet Union (or USSR) was a socialist country.

In those days of the cold war, each nation was against what the other stood for either good or bad, and Angola which was a struggling nation in Central Africa and seeking her independence despite being very rich in oil and natural gas became the playground for the ugly politics of the super powers.

Even if the Super Powers were right, for the sake of everything they represented, Capitalism to the Americans and Socialism for the Soviet Union, they stood against each other as a result of the unending political disagreements. The hopes of many developing nations for an egalitarian society were dashed or prolonged and Angola's march towards independence was one of them. It was very sad.

The disagreement between Africa's largest concentration of black people Nigeria and the United States of America, the Super power, marked a new shift from the foreign policy of Nigeria from moderate policy of General Gowon to active participation in African affairs during the regime of General Muritala Mohammed.

However, the story here was not about America and Nigeria complications, it was the creation of seven new States by military fiat in 1976. It was the events that shaped and created a policy of manipulation and frustration among the people, who according to traditional history in West Africa had created independence from each other through wars and mutual respect from the time of old or defunct Oyo Empire that preceded the advent of British colonization in Africa.

The State of Ogun was one of three new States that came out of the old Western State, that very action of the Federal Military Government merged Nigeria's two powerful and ruthless ethnic groups among the Yoruba tribes into a single State.

The Federal Government out of ignorance or otherwise for the history of the two powerful Yoruba sub-ethnic groups named the State after the river that flows almost entirely, within the domain of one group. (Egba) though in future, the other section tried to change the name of the new State to Gateway State to reflect commonality, but it was resisted by every political force known to man in that part of the world and that would be one of the themes for the foundation of this book.

However, unknown to the Federal Government of Nigeria, pride was the ego that was altered from inception from the name of the State to other groups. It was like a form of colonization to the non Egba in the State.

The rumor and interest for the details of the additional States creation in Nigeria from the twelve it was, in 1967 with an additional seven in 1976. The location of the State capital was not immediately known to the "Owambe" (a party loving people of Abeokuta, the City noted for producing and drinking only "Top Beer" from a brewery factory located in the City of the Egba) by late Chief Lawson.

However, the creation and the interest of a new State was not a major factor, they assumed by standard of using the old administrative provinces parameter left behind by the British, that Egba State would be a given. But the politics behind the closed door was a different ball game altogether.

The Irekefe panel which was set up by the Federal Government of Nigeria under late Genera Muritala Mohammed for the creation of new States did not produce a document the Egba wanted or viewed.

Everybody knew, from history about the events that led to the collapse of the old Oyo Empire and how the Empire was almost replaced by another power conclave called Ibadan warriors including Yoruba war tactically called Kiriji, before the country was colonized by the British, the Ijebu and Egba operated a cat and mouse relationship. Both with highly educated Yoruba ethnics had interests in business and a social lifestyle in Lagos and Ibadan.

The distrust among them could be seen or felt like the current and shocks of electriCity. It was the way of life then, keep your adversaries at arm's length was the policy adopted by the two provinces.

Inter-marriages were sometimes viewed as crossing the line between all they stood for. In most cases both of them were never truly loved in Ibadan, the then Capital of the Western Region and the City which retained the capital of the new Oyo State.

Furthermore, the people of Ibadan on the other hand that played host to these two old provinces of Ijebu and Egba for decades, was the capital of the old Western State for many centuries often made uncomplimentary jokes about the Ijebu, including their mixed feelings for the political activities of the late Chief Obafemi Awolowo.

The Ibadan hard feelings ran very deep in politics. The social life and any inter-marriage with any Ijebu was always a hard nut to crack or a project to sell in the sixties and seventies to other Yoruba. Nothing but envy and lack of understanding about what made the Egba and Ijebu stronger and more prosperous could be responsible for the hostilities to these powerful Yoruba ethnic groups.

The deep suspicions and lack of understanding of this sub-ethnic group of the Yoruba tribe was so bad that people of Ibadan would jokingly say "If you see an Ijebu man and a snake at the same time, the better option would be to kill the Ijebu man first. If you fail to do this on time, you will probably be killed by the Ijebu before the first bite of the snake."

The other Yoruba ethnic groups often misunderstood the Ijebu group, who were traditionally astute economists. They love to save and invest in the future more than any group in Nigeria, they continue to build their political and economic perceptiveness on backward integrations and they are as ruthless and as astute as the Igbo tribe in the Eastern part of Nigeria.

There was an unconfirmed story about a rich Ijebu man who cooked a nice meal of fish, but would eat around the fish and put it back in the pot for another presentation to the public the next day who assumed he was eating well.

There were many unusual economic stories about life among the tribes of Nigeria about Ijebu, but in fact, they were not truthful and were but based on assumptions and inability to understand the goals and plans of the Ijebu.

The history of the State could also be traced back to 1967, when Lagos State was created out of old Western Region. Nigeria went from four regions to twelve States by General Yakubu Gowon, the youngest Head of State in Nigeria. His plan then, was to weaken and discourage the secession interest of the Igbo or Biafra in Eastern Nigeria which Col. Emeka Ojukwu led for almost 30 months.

Egba comprised of the people from Abeokuta and its surrounding traditional towns and villages. They lost the bulk of their potential Civil Service men and women in other cities in the western Region to Lagos State in 1967.

They stayed behind with the new Lagos State government because of proximity to Abeokuta, while the majority of the Ijebu moved to Ibadan.

By the time Ogun State was created out of the Western State in 1976, Ijebu automatically had the bulk of the Civil Service and Egba were by definition, a minority in a new State which they had the State Capital City (Abeokuta) which had no meaningful impact on the thinking and performance of the government through the new Civil Service.

The politics of survival became the bedrock of a State that was yet to have a serious foundation in development. It was bad and very unfortunate. It could not be confirmed, but it was said that the Ijebu cried foul played on them by the Egba and the emergence of Abeokuta as the capital of the new State in 1976.

General Olusegun Obasanjo who was then the Chief of Staff Supreme Headquarters and Madam Ajoke Muritala Mohammed, the wife of the Head of State, were indigenes of Abeokuta, and were silently accused to have influenced the location of the new State capital.

Rumor had it, that the State capital was first slated for the City of Sagamu in the Remo ethnic group by the Irekefe panel that recommended the new State. But Ijebu felt they could not work with the Remo or allow the Capital to be located in a City which by tradition, was beneath the level of Ijebu Ode or that of Awujale, the paramount ruler of the Ijebu land.

However, it was in the process of in-fighting between the Ijebu and Remo people (over the location of the State Capital) that the Egba realized their province was going to be grouped with the Ijebu and Remo in a new State. Innocently, the Egba had expected their separate State, to be named after the river in their City or called Ogun/Yewa because of the Egbado.

Why would anyone imagine the unification would not be seen as unequally yoking, the mixed ideas and goals was beyond law and rational reasoning?

The new State by previous calculations would have benefited the Egba only in name, but not with the seat of government. If the City of Sagamu in Remoland was adopted as the seat of the government, (but as fate would have it) Abeokuta the political headquarters of Egbaland was made the new State capital by the Federal Military government.

Unfortunately, most of the workers in the new Civil Service were not from Abeokuta or Egba, technically, the Egba became a minority group in the Civil Service of the new State. It was like having a car with no legs to drive it and asking your tradition rival in previous years to be the driver and that was the situation for the Egba in 1976 as the Ijebu became the drivers of the new State.

The Ijebu made jokes about the predicament the Egba were in and described Abeokuta as only a State capital on the administrative document of the new State without anything to show for it. It was a sad beginning for the Ijebu and Abeokuta provinces.

All five traditional Egba groups, Ibara, Owu, Ake, Gbagura and Oke-Ana became united under the leadership of the most respected King of Egbaland, the late Oba Oyebade Lipede the Alake of Egbaland for the tasks ahead.

The Strategy on how to handle the new problem at hand would be different from how the old war was fought and won with the support of the British, it would be a battle of brain than physical, and the Egba would have to do it all alone.

The system of traditional administration of Egba was different from other Yoruba groups; Abeokuta was more of a political City, for all Egba, none of the five groups could claim sole ownership or control of the City and the surrounding villages and towns all took their directives from the five kings located in the City of Abeokuta.

Unconfirmed stories said it was indeed the late King Oyebade Lipede who persuaded General Obasanjo and the wife of the then Head of State, Mrs. Ajoke Muritala Mohammed to make sure the State Capital was located in Abeokuta, the ancient historical City of the Egba, whose people are still referred to as "Omo Lisabi".

The new State created a platform for the unity the Egba wanted before they were merged with Nigeria. Perhaps similar to the aroo unification policy of Lisabi Agbongbo Akala before the old Oyo Empire was defeated.

A bit of this story on the larger than life influences of the late Oba Lipede was referred to by this writer in a published article years ago that can be found at Nigeriaworld.com and other newspapers in 2005 when Oba Lipede died. It was titled *"How Oba Lipede Restored the Glory of Egba Land"*

However, the new Ogun State created mixed feelings of sadness and joy for different people. The Egba rejoiced for the location of the State Capital in their domain, but regretted the problems that were ahead in working with their traditional adversaries dated back to the period of defunct old Oyo Empire, the Ijebu on the other hand, never liked it either.

How can we serve the Ibadan for years under the dispensation of old Western State and serve the Egba in a new indulgence of Ogun State? That was a bitter pill for them to swallow.

Subsequently, both of them re-opened the primitive wars files fought over one hundred years ago, instead of facing the future with hope they looked at each again as enemies. It was a very sad relationship.

The Ijebu at one time almost rewrote their history about the fact that they were not originally Yoruba or descendants of Oduduwa. Their paramount ruler, the highly respected Awujale of Ijebuland Oba Sikiru Adetona who became King at the age of 26, later in life wrote how the Ijebu originated from Whydah in Saudi Arabia, a fact which the late Gov. Bisi Onabanjo described as a sign of frustration on the part of the King, because they belonged to different political parties.

Somehow, if one could examine closely the behavior of his people among the Yoruba group, the King might in fact have been right. The Ijebu were special and a different brand of the Yoruba race in terms of culture and social life: They were more organized and economically resourceful and prudent to the point of miserly. It is the truth the Egba or the Yoruba nation will have to admit.

However, the minorities in the new State like Remo and Egbado now called Yewa and Awori were not only mentally and emotional deflated but their fears on the future were written all over their faces.

To be in the same camp and cage of Nigeria's foremost oppressors, the Egba and Ijebu; the two most ruthless ethic groups among the Yoruba was to give up on any reasonable and unreasonable ambitions. That means they could only get the leftovers of Egba and Ijebu. If there was anything left at all because both were selfish and ruthless on the policy of even distribution of amenities.

However, between the two, the Egba would be a better choice and a more understandable senior colleague than the Ijebu to the minorities in the State. It was like your doctor asking you to choose between Colon Cancer and Parkinson disease, neither of the two had any survival strategies except for the life span of Parkinson disease over Cancer.

Ogun State from the beginning was consumed with fear, distrust and lack of direction unlike other new States created in 1976.

How will the new State turn negative diversity into strength and progress?

Nigerians from all walks of life, particularly from the other two States that came out of the Western State (Oyo and Ondo) were equally watching the development of events in the new State called Ogun with captivated attention.

How can the two traditional and historical opponents be friends who out of self-determination before the introduction of the British colonization led to the end of the Oyo Kingdom?

Will they use voodoo on each other like they did in the Old Oyo Empire during the battle of Kiriji. Those were the unanswered questions on the minds of all.

In fact, most students who knew the political and economic history of Nigeria were surprised at the unreasonable unification of the group by the Federal Government of Nigeria. It was the greatest mistake of the Irekefe panel on the State creation, which may never be corrected by any simple method.

However, the new Oyo State felt relieved at the departure of the Ijebu and Egba from Ibadan City because of factors ranging from the inordinate ambition of the two and keen competition with unholy alliances of minds and purposes: Their departure from Ibadan would open up opportunities for promotions, they believed.

Also, separation of the duo from old the Western State was also a bundle of joy for the oppressed people of the new Ondo State which comprised of the ethnic groups of the Ekitis, Ondo and others, with Akure City as the Capital of the Ondo State.

If the Ekitis had questions for the Irekefe panel on the State creation or wanted Ado Ekiti as the Capital they never openly questioned the rationale behind Irekefe's panel selection of Akure as the capital. Unlike the Ijebu in Ogun State, it was a battle the Ekiti in Ondo State had to fight several years later, in a more polite way than the Ijebu of Ogun State that was before Ado Ekiti became the Capital of a new Ekiti State under General Sanni Abacha in 1996 almost 20 years later.

Ondo State despite their education as the group with the largest concentration of Ph.D. holders in Nigeria, They lagged behind in everything. The new State was the first to produce Nigeria's first Professor of Mathematics Prof. Adegoke Olubumno long before independence, a new State to them was assumed to be a kind of freedom and opportunities for growth like it was for the Oyo State: But in Ogun State it was the reopening of the suspended primitive war files before the arrival of the British colonization of the country.

Indeed all Nigerians were more interested in Ogun State events than any other six new States created in 1976. In fact, in years to come they were not disappointed because the Egba and Ijebu unleashed on each other the greatest attack and political maneuvers ever known in Nigeria: The use of voodoo on each other, including political executions and murders in unbelievable manners was revealed as events unfolded.

Ogun State by definition is in the south western part of Nigeria in West Africa and borders on the South by Lagos State, Oyo and Oshun State in the North, Ondo State in the East and Republic of Benin in the West: The economic gateway to the rest of West African countries.

What happened to the internal politics of the State's Civil Service, and how Ijebu and Egba tried to overcome hatred, for respect of each ethnic group in a State, that was built on distrust and complete disregard for the rule of law and nepotism?

"He who wishes to serve his country must have not only the power to think, but the will to act"

Plato

Awa lo mo Abeokuta, ilu rere ilu olola, Ilu to duro lase oluwa, Egba omo Lisabi

Chief Ebenezer Obe Fabiyi

Ijebu Omo Alaaren, Omo Afidi pote mole

Ita ntebo ni IjebuOde.

Anonymou.s

2

ACTIVITIES

What were the activities of various Governors in the State since 1976 to all the political imbroglios, between the Egba and Ijebu while the minorities like the Awori and Egbado now called Yewa and Remo became onlookers in a State where they were supposed to be active participants? How come, none of the minorities were strong enough to ask questions?

Again, it was like the minorities in the State were helplessly in a cage, the cage of Ijebu and Egba. The Egba became the beneficiary of the new State capital without the resources to manage or control the events that would have given them a befitting State Capital or the spread of infrastructural development to other Egba towns and villages. It was like attempting to drive a car without any brakes on a freeway which was what happened.

They had no senior members in the new State Civil Service to influence the thinking of the government. The first military Governor Col. Ayodele Balogun was not even an indigene of Ogun State, but he was married to an Ijebu woman (was then the rumor.)

There was no official confirmation of it, which was the information available then. It made his administration subject to effective remote control and manipulations from his in-laws and the Awujale palace, the paramount ruler of the Ijebu people was equally the assumption.

Perhaps, the leadership style of the first Governor of the State was a suspect, but it served the immediate objectives and tactics of the Ijebu at the detriment of others in the State: The Egba would be an administrative State capital on paper while the bulk of development would be in Ijebu areas of the State as events would reveal in the future.

The first Military Governor was faced with chronic accommodations and office spaces for the new government; Abeokuta was not a prepared society for the new and explosive development the new State was coming with. Most civil servants were still commuting from Ibadan to work in Abeokuta every day: It was tough on the Government and people.

That was the foundation and blueprint of the managers of the new State, the trust and sincerity was lost at the foundation of the new State, it was the beginning of policy of frustration and manipulation in the State.

The above scenario, describes the political and social given conditions among the Ijebu powerful group: Though the Egba were also equal to the tasks and strategies of the new State in the politics of manipulation and frustration, both treated each other like cat and mouse in meetings which were often held in an atmosphere of distrust and unreasonable checks and balances.

The covenant that would have united them as a State that could compete effectively and positively with Lagos State in terms of development was tactically broken at its foundation in 1976.

The task to draft Egba sons and daughters from every part of the country and abroad to the new State Civil Service was a massive project embraced by the late Alake of Egba Land Oba Oyebade Lipede was later in life described by this writer as the best monarch the Egba ever had.

The Royal Highness Oba Lipede spoke directly to anyone who wanted to listen and he encouraged his people to come "Home" regularly. The level of secrecy often associated with the palace in the past decades was reduced and he opened it to all his subjects called "Egba Omo Lisabi".

Some of the highly placed Egba sons like my boss the late Femi Sowoolu, the Director of National Achieves at Ibadan situated inside the University of Ibadan campus rejected the plea of the King to leave his Federal position to descend to a local or State position. He however, offered logistics and upward search for new graduates to work at the State level.

Many were given unknown friendly or funny chieftaincy titles unknown to the history and tradition of the Egba and the joy of being a Chief in the Palace of the King could be seen on the faces all: No matter how funny or strange the title was, the only condition from the King was the recipient of the Chieftaincy title had to have a decent resident in the City of Abeokuta: It was a simple and easy condition for most of the money bags sons and daughters of the Kingdom lost to Ibadan, Lagos, the rest of the country and beyond.

Abeokuta was gradually shedding the hostile environment it had in the past to a conducive business one for all, not only the Egba, but all who cared, they have transform the outward hospitality to what grow the City of their ancestors.

Oba Lipede had an open display of affection and open love for his people. Most of the time he consulted with the other four kings in the City before he moved on with any program from the Palace.

Abeokuta was the City my father relocated me to in 1969 when he refused to allow me to continue my education in Ibadan due to my association with defiant friends in the City in 1968 after graduating from St. Bridges Primary School Mokola Ibadan.

Late teacher Akindele of St. Paul Primary School Igbore knew how to handle defiant teenager, and the late Mr. Agunbiade of **Agunbiade Victory High** was directly my primary six grade teacher, who made us to act our first play," **The Merchant of Venice**" It's a tragic comedy by William Shakespeare, believed to have been written between 1596 and 1598.

Though the play was classified as a comedy in sharing certain aspects with Shakespeare's other romantic comedies, the play is perhaps most remembered for its dramatic scenes, and is best known for Shylock and the famous 'Hath not a Jew eyes' speech. Also notable is Portia's speech about the 'quality of mercy'.

I played the role of Bassanio, Antonio's friend who was in love with Portia. Portia, which was played by Adenike Johnson who later in my infatuated childish life became my girlfriend until we both realized that the childhood play was not the real life when she went to Abeokuta Grammar School in 1970.

Abeokuta City's belief system was both modern and traditional. All faiths were respected and each was located next to each other, meaning, Church, Mosques and Egungun shrines could be seen on the same street. My custodian house was almost opposite Ile *Ogboni* secluded shrine at Isale Igbein in Abeokuta with a tall Iroko tree on which the famous Egungun "Ajeran" masquerade used to emerge in those days.

Muslims and Christians could be seen flirting with Egungun followers or disciples at each other's festivals. In fact, we had a saying that the belief in Jesus Christ or Islamic faith should not influence a person's belief in traditional gods.

To the Egba, all religions belonged to one God and they are all struggling for the expansion of their congregational database of followers, with that assumption, the Egba were able to create tolerance and respect for all religions, long before other tribes in Nigeria.

The religious tolerance of Egba dated way back to the misunderstanding with the missionaries and the British which tried to abolish African religion because of Christianity but they were surprised the Egba sent them packing with their Bibles until they accepted the condition that Christianity must never interfere with the custom and religion of the fore fathers of the Egba if they planned to stay in the kingdom to practice their religion of Holy Trinity.

I remember how I met the Alake of Egbaland Oba Oyebade Lipede in his palace in 1986: I was searching for a job and it was not uncommon in those days to seek the support of whoever could press the button for you sadly, I had none. I went to the King and he was there for me just like he did for many of my generations in his time as the King of Egbaland.

Uncle Fajol of Fajol Hotels and real estate business in the City and Princess Bisi Gbadebo the sister of current Alake of Egbaland Oba Adedotun Gbadebo, at a time she was a onetime Registrar of Federal Agriculture University in Abeokuta who had arranged a meeting for me to meet the King.

When Kabiyesi Oba Lipede peeped through the window of his two- story building to see me, I did my best to understand the Yoruba tradition on how the elders are greeted. I went down and prostrated as much I could because of his location and distance.

"You need to give a full prostration," his palace guard thundered.

It was the custom of the Yoruba to prostrate on the floor with ones chest close to the floor when you greet a King.

"That is okay, leave my child alone, and be nice in your approach to this new generation," the King said in a very assuring voice.

"Kabiyesi!" the guard responded as was the custom.

The New Alake's Palace was beautiful. It was parallel to the old one and it had all the paraphernalia's of the traditions of the Egba. It had decorations of symbols of the might and strength of the Egba Kingdom, dating back to the period preceding the British colonization of Nigeria.

It was a fearless Kingdom merged with Nigeria in 1914, Abeokuta City had witnessed many developments from positive to negative and sometimes unhappy memories, but the new generation would be amazed at the complete display of ignorance and backward slashes of the former harbor of the freed slaves in 1830.

There was a time when the City had a King named Oba Ademola, whose actions out of wisdom or otherwise robbed the Kingdom of the location of the first university by the British government in the country in 1948 because of infinitesimal issues, over closeness of Rev. Ransom Kuti the Chairman of the panel for the university location to the former slave masters the British or land allocation which the King purportedly wanted to deal directly with the British Government.

The reason for it could not be ascertained. It was the age of rumor. They said it was because the King was interested in the wife of the Chairman of the panel who was a social critic of his authority and women's rights.

What a missed opportunity for a project as gigantic as the University of Ibadan which was followed years later with the over imposing University Teaching Hospital UCH and the impact of it on Abeokuta or Egba community?

Whatever it was, it led the monarchy to abdicate the throne for Ile Ife City over taxes and rights of women including other domestic politics of the Egba Kingdom: In a social struggle led by the most respected late Madam Funmilayo Ransom Kuti the mother of the three musketeers Late Professor Olikoye Kuti, Fela Anikulapo Kuti and Dr. Beko Kuti.

However, the Kingdom suffered from lack of development and most indigenes stayed away from Abeokuta. When they did come, it was to attend parties or funerals of loved ones for few hours.

It should never be forgotten how generous the Oba Oyebade Lipede was to his people: As a student of Lisabi Grammar School in the City of Abeokuta in the early seventies, I knew how ugly things were and how hostile the past was.

There were various ritual killings of women and children with primitive sacrifices to most blood sucking demons all in the name of spiritual worship of local deities. Those of us in the school hostels were scared to interact with the City because of ritual killings, and our teachers told us negative stories to keep us indoor.

However, the period under Oba Lipede was different. He was a polished and educated King. His ever shining shoes and tradition "Irukere" were majestic to behold. He was almost 6 feet tall, a king that walked with the grace of his office and lots of money in his pocket, his people was told he was a successful Ship magnate.

Unlike others before him, the King had the look of a leader one could trust any time. His people trusted him with the destiny of the Kingdom and Oba Oyebade Lipede never failed them for thirty three years he reigned over Egbaland.

Before the ascension of the Alake of Egbaland in 1972, Abeokuta City, despite being the first City to adopt western education in Nigeria, it had just eleven secondary schools with most of the successful and respected graduates and future leaders emerging from Baptist Boys High school and Abeokuta Grammar school.

Those two institutions had a two-year HSC advanced level education programs for direct entry into the three Universities located in old western State. They were the University of Ibadan, University of Ife and University of Lagos. (*"How Oba Lipede Restored the Glory of Egbaland" by this writer published by Nigeriaworld.com.*)

One of the respected secondary schools then was Lisabi Grammar School which this author attended. It also produced Pastor Tunde Bakare of Later Rain Church: The other schools were Reverend Kuti Memorial Grammar School, Macjob Grammar School, Abeokuta Girls High School, St. Peter's College, Egba High School, and Ebenezer High School. All of them served as feeder schools to those two institutions with advanced level programs.

The control and academic dominance of these two with Advanced Level or HSC programs were often challenged in the field of sports by Lisabi Grammar School and St. Peter College which also had intention to set up advanced level programs but they lost out to the internal politics from old Western State capital then at Ibadan.

The bulk of the future leaders of what became the bedrock of Egba presentations to the new Ogun State Civil Service in 1976 came from all these schools and those that migrated from Ibadan after the State was created.

My father came from Ibadan to enjoy the benefits of the new State creations that freed him and his generation from stagnancy in promotions which aided his rapid growth in his career as a civil servant like all his generation.

Interestingly, the rivalry of the internal Egba traditional five Councils of Oba's, Owu, Ake, Ibara, Gbagura, and Oke Ona were suspended for the unity of the Egba under the leadership of Late Oba Oyebade Mofolunso Lipede the Alake of Egbaland. It was a forced unity with common goals for the Egba to come together to fight for a common interest to the continued existence and progress of the group that first brought western civilization to Nigeria, within the micro unit of Ogun State.

The people that first exposed Nigeria to press freedom with the publication of "Iwe Iroyin" by Rev. Henry Townsend in Abeokuta between 1846 to 1867, He based his mission in the City according to Ajisafe. He was the second European to enter the City of Abeokuta in 1843 after Thomas Birch Freeman did in the period of Sodeke, Henry Townsend in collaboration with Samuel Ajai Crowder who later became a Bishop educationally placed Abeokuta ahead of any Yoruba community.

They both translated most of the English Hymns to Yoruba language perhaps the press freedom in their time through the newspapers that was established was the second of its kind since Lisabi Agbongbo Akala united the Egba together through his Aaroo policy to ward off the control of Alaafin of Old Oyo Empire in the 19th century. Nothing could be more important to the Egba than individual freedom or personal liberty.

However, unlike the Egba in the new State, the road map to the State creation was more of a prepared and organized journey for the Ijebu than the Egba. Every infrastructure was in place for them, the Civil Services, the social associations based on age and cities, secret meetings and manipulation of events made the Ijebu more closely united than the Egba. It was a closed, woven political rope which was cleverly wrapped, in the unity of the Ijebu "alaaren" which was a revelation to the much surprised Egba.

Subsequently, the above scenario would be a challenge for the Egba to penetrate in years to come. On top of that, the leadership of the paramount ruler of the Ijebu people [Awujale of Ijebuland] was never in dispute. Unlike that of Alake of Egbaland which was based on respect. That of Ijebu was unquestionably built upon history, tradition and also controlled by the spiritual unity of the Agemo group with their yearly celebrated "Ojude Oba" festivals which further marked the authority and homage of the Ijebu to Awujale by all Ijebu.

Furthermore, like the Egba, their new partners in the State were ruthless and very aggressive, they loved their people and towns more than any Yoruba race could imagine. Before an Ijebu man could erect or buy any property or invest anywhere in Nigeria or overseas, he had to start from "home".

Like they say, charity begins at home and ends abroad. The Ijebu unity and the love could be seen from the affection and loyalty to their cities due to the commitment and dedication to growth of the community.

If an Ijebu daughter wanted to build or acquire a property in Ijebu land, she would manipulate her husband to do that first for her. To this group among the Yoruba tribe, a house was more than just a place to sleep. It must have provision for everything like a big yard for social events or parties.

In other words, while the Egba architectural style was conservative like the British, the Ijebu style was massive, like Americans. The only way to describe the architectural styles of the two in the events before the State creation or it could be compared to properties in Brooklyn, New York in terms of space to that of spacious and massive City of Dallas, in Texas.

Moreover, it was rumored then that, if married Ijebu daughters were given plots of land to erect buildings in any area of Ijebu City, their names were solely on the Certificate of occupancy not the husbands unless both were Ijebu.

From a bird's eye view, most of the Ijebu towns had a better metropolitan outlook than the Egba. All which remained faced the challenges ahead for the people of "Owambe" that produced top Nigerians and Africans artists like, Yusuf Olatunji, Fela Anikulapo Kuti, Ebenezer Obey, Prince Adekunle, Idowu Animashaun, Uncle Toye Ajagun, Shina Peters and Tunji Oyelana in the seventies.

The Ijebu like the Egba owned the choice properties in Lagos and Ibadan especially around Bodija, Oke Bola, Challenge Molete and all the South East of Ibadan.

At one time, most of the landed properties at Kuto Areas of Abeokuta were all almost owned by the foresighted Ijebu.

During that period, the Egba were becoming increasingly worried about how to handle these very aggressive businessmen and women in the new State when they realized that they had to buy properties from Ijebu in Abeokuta their own City.

It was almost an insult to the integrity and business expertise of the Egba, which made them look inward to business activities in Egbaland.

New businesses like real estate companies owned by Ijebu were then visible in the New State Capital until Chief Jolaosho, an Egba and confidant of Alake of Abeokuta decided to match the new encroachers in the real estate business. He started the Fajol Real Estate and other chains of Investment like Fajol Hotels and most of the Egba started to invest at "home" unlike the traditional Egba gravel and sharp supply business to Lagos. A new look at how investment and manufacturing could become part of a thinking faculty of the people emerged.

The Abeokuta Club was the arrow head of development and politics of the Egba the other entire social clubs in Abeokuta or Egba had their patrons from Abeokuta Club. At one time the late Engineer Yomi Adenekan, a former Director in the State's Ministry of Works who was one of the executives of the Club was delegated with the special duty to recruit Egba indigenes from Lagos to join the club.

It was strictly a mandate from his Royal Highness Oba Oyebade Lipede and other Kings of Egba towns to fish out all Egba in Lagos and Ibadan or anywhere to come "Home".

I can still recall the day I was on a business trip to discuss "Form M" with the Federal Ministry of Finance and Central Bank of Nigeria (CBN) on behalf of Gateway Pharmaceutical Company and I met Chief Bunmi Sowande, a Chartered Accountant with Coopers and Lybrand in Lagos. He was from Abeokuta but grew up in Lagos. I got him to sign up as a member of the Abeokuta Club.

At the time late Chief MKO Abiola established the first major football club in Abeokuta. It was named Abiola Babes. We had no befitting stadium except the Asero Stadium and Ijeja Stadium which was converted to a basketball practicing center.

Abiola Babes needed good footballers to join the team: I was very close to Best Ogedegbe and Muda Lawal of the IICC Shooting Stars FC in my days at Ekotedo Ibadan, Omoniyi who was the goalkeeper for UBA FC, Moses who use to play for Water Corporation also at Ibadan, along with Segun Odegbami, who was a good friend of Sunday Oladele, called Laadoo, who became President of Yaba Tech, both of them had attended Ibadan Polytechnic for the Ordinary National Diploma programs in

Engineering. All of them were my friends at Ekotedo when I was a staff of the National Bank at Agodi branch at Ibadan: The task of facilitating these players to leave IICC Shooting Stars for Abiola Babes was given to me.

My friend Bayo Somuyiwa now in Brighton Canada and I organized a football match through my company Rolex Organization; we invited Water Corporation FC of Ibadan to play against Abiola Babes at Asero Stadium. We did not make any profit because the security was compromised by the police, but we achieved our objective to place Abeokuta on the interstate football map later it was very easy to invite some of the players to join the Babes in Abeokuta.

It was the performance of Abiola Babes in the National League and Challenge Cup which the team won twice that made the government of Brigadier Popoola to lay the foundation for the MKO Abiola Stadium.

The final of the Challenge Cup in Lagos between the Leventist united and Abiola Babes was the most significant event though the Babes lost the game, it was the first time Lagosians saw how Tippers loaders were used to bring the Egbas to the Stadium and when the final whistle came the Egba could not believe the game was over and that Abiola Babes lost, the press made a big deal out of the ignorance of the Egba on the pages of the papers next day.

The press was funny they wrote uncomplimentary stories on how the people of Ogun State thought the match was going to be replayed after the referee's blew the last whistle because the ninety minutes game went too fast with Abiola Babes losing the game maybe the press was right as most people from Abeokuta particularly the Tipper loaders cried like babes. We wanted the Cup badly if it was just to say thank you to MKO Abiola for all his contributions even to our King the pillar of the hope of modern Egba nation.

It was sad.

Years later, I assembled investors for the establishment of Obantoko Community Bank with Alhaji Nurudeen Oyedele who became a Permanent Secretary in the Governor's office, late Mrs. Martins the mother of the Arch Bishop Martins in Lagos, Engineer Oni, Sobande of the Peat Marwick Accounting firm in Lagos, Sunday Elijah the Chief Accountant of Niger Cedar Industries Ikeja Lagos, late Mr. Sobode a onetime permanent Secretary with the State Ministry of Works and son-in-law to Mrs. Martins, Aibana based in

New York, and others, due to logistics and take off grants we merged the Bank with investors from Ogun State Polytechnic, with 40 % ownership through the recommendation of Alhaji Nurudeen Oyedele and it was relocated to the main campus of Ogun State Polytechnic.

It was a joy for me to see, the microfinance Bank in the Polytechnic was my idea, and I got the license for the Obantoko before the merger because Ogun State Polytechnic was denied a license by the Central Bank of Nigeria.

Whatever the balance of my shares, along with other investors, I got involved in the Community Bank like late Mr. Sobode, the late Mrs. Martins the mother of Arch Bishop Martins of Catholic dioceses Lagos, Sowande of Coopers and Lybrand Sunny Elijah, Abiodun Osomo, Engineer Oni, Col Olusegun Atanda, and Aibana a physical therapist in New York was not disclosed till today.

Maybe one day someone will ask a question on what happened to their investments in Obantoko Community Bank which was merged with Ogun Polytechnic with 40 % ownership. So far no information was given but the bank continues to grow on the sweat of other people without respect for decency or returns for those who initially conceived the project.

It was sad.

I also got my childhood friend Segun Oni, a structural Engineer to quit his private sector job in Lagos to join the services of Ogun State local government. We all wanted to develop Ogun State in a way Abeokuta or the Egba will not be left behind.

Despite the western education of the Egba, all the four local governments that were located in the Egba areas by 1979, only Abeokuta looked like a City. Others were glorified villages pretending to be cities, but they were not even towns.

The possibilities of Abeokuta and other smaller towns and villages to grow into metropolitan cities were limited because of the traditional set-up of Egba institutions.

All five Egba Obas by tradition wanted to be in Abeokuta City, while the other towns and villages were under the control of "Baales". They had to report to each King in Abeokuta, depending on their set up.

It was not the same among the Ijebu. Each City had its own paramount ruler, chosen on mutual respect and complete love for the community. The Ijebu had more community support and programs than the Egba. It was a political game the Egba had to learn in the years to come to work as a team. If they were able to meet the challenges ahead; otherwise, they would have been left behind like a bad habit in the State.

Furthermore, the Awujale of Ijebu land had more support from educated and polished Kings; he could go to any negotiation table to confront the Egba than the paramount ruler of the Egba. It was politics 101; The Kabiyesi Oba Oyebade had to learn on how to improve the Egba traditional council. Graciously the Alake realized this and he planned to reform his Council.

Alake embarked on reforming the Egba traditional Council to meet the challenges ahead through elevation of local Baales to third class tradition of Oba. However, Oba Tejuosho, the Oshinle of Oke Onaland and a trained medical doctor was a pain for "Baba" as the Alake was also called.

Oba Tejuoso created a lot of problems for the Alake. Like questioning how the supremacy of Alake could be assumed when the facts of history did not support it.

The tales of oral traditional history often referred to by Oba Tejuosho were questionable to those who would not dare question the leadership of Alake. In most cases, his tales were often ignored by those not interested in the past. But how to move Egba nation in progressive direction like the Ijebu within the new State and the process adopted by the Oshinle of Oke Onaland Oba Tejuosho almost destroyed the fragile unity the State creation brought to the Egba.

Can we blame His Royal Highness Oba Tejuosho if he elects to defend his heritage? Do we expect him to slaughter facts of history for the sake of Unity? Which of the five Egba came first to Abeokuta, who among them should be the leader?

However, the supremacy of the Alake over other Kings in Egbaland had been established several decades, it had become immemorial and questioning it now will destroy the fragile unity of the Egba which was consolidated since Lisabi liberated them from Old Oyo Empire, that however, became the questions and problems for the new Egba in the 20th Century.

Oba Tejuosho was tactically rebuffed to accept the leadership of Alake or lose relevancy by all the members in the Abeokuta Club. Gladly he did what he had to do, to maintain his place as first among equals, honestly, it did not affect his status and the people united behind the leadership of Alake of Egbaland because of the task of building Egba nation with Ogun State superseded the micro interest of the sub unit of Egba community.

Apart from the Abeokuta Club, new social clubs emerged in every part of the City to unite and encourage the upcoming Egba. Such as; the Abeokuta Socialite Club, Lisabi Elites and many others were based on age and affluence in the country but the link with Abeokuta club was the unity for all clubs which became the pool for their patrons.

The Abeokuta Club was the mother for all those clubs and was closely followed by Lisabi Elites and the Abeokuta Social Elites for the youths and young graduates in the Civil Service.

The objectives then were to assist and motivate each other not to give up on most of the Civil Service positions held. Most of the first line senior officers were Ijebu that operated a policy of frustration to drive away the few Egba in the service. It was a political chess game the Egba had to learn quickly and we did.

Politics in the State was based on manipulation. It was a cat and mouse relationship. Some Egba in the Civil Service had no link with some of the social clubs because they felt they about local politics, they paid dearly the price for their carelessness. They became victims of Ijebu ruthless policy because they forgot all politic are local.

Those who could not stand the heat in the kitchen left the Civil Service out of frustration, despite their initial positive contributions and enthusiasms to the development of the new State in 1976.

However, most of the clubs in Egba were labeled secret societies by the Ijebu to create division of its fragile unity. They often planted spies in the clubs who pretended to be Egba.

All these sometimes led to dismissal or resignation from the Civil Service. There was a secret code among the Egba not to discuss details with your wife at home, if she happened to be an Ijebu woman.

Somehow, the Egba never gave up, they hung in there. They were in a State that had the potential to be the best but could not because of the above scenarios, they refused to give up.

A few months after the seven States were created, General Muritala Mohammed the Nigeria Head of State was murdered in Lagos. In an unsuccessful military Coup by Col Buka Suka Dimka and soldiers loyal to the former Head of State General Gowon and General Bissala a member of the Supreme Military Council, General Obasanjo his deputy became the new Nigeria Head of State with the approval of the Supreme Military Council.

Interestingly, the first Military Governor of the State was removed within the period of two years in July 1978. Colonel Harris Eghagha became the new State administrator and he instituted a preparatory transition program to hand over government to a civilian administration headed by General Obasanjo as planned by the late General Muritala Mohammed.

Subsequently, in 1978, all the Ogun State indigenes admitted into Ibadan Polytechnics were told to leave by the Oyo State government because the previous government under Colonel Balogun did not remit the two hundred thousand naira administrative running costs for the institution.

As a result 25-28 % of students' admission allocation to the State could no longer be sustained on goodwill of the Oduduwa connection or Yoruba solidarity. It takes money to buy whiskey like they say in Texas in the United States of America, in other words, it takes money to run any institution of higher learning like the Polytechnic.

Two hundred thousand naira was a lot of money in those days when the Nigeria Currency, naira was stronger than the United States of America's dollars. It was a sad situation for this writer, and many others who had resigned their appointments for school admission at Ibadan Polytechnic only to be sent packing due to the two States imbroglio.

About fifty of us from Ibadan travelled by road and together we marched to the office of Brigadier Harris Eghagha, the new administrator in Abeokuta to open up dialogue with the Oyo State government. It was at the meeting held at Ibara's office of the Commissioner of Education that the decision to establish a Polytechnic in Ogun State was recommended, instead of the policy to fund the school at Ibadan which we had only 25-28% student admission allocation.

The recommendation for the new Ogun State Polytechnic was adopted by the government with a military decree as the State Polytechnic became a reality, however instead of the state to rejoice over the new creation, instead the politics of frustration and location of the new institution came up again.

The Ijebu wanted the Polytechnic in Ijebu Ode as a compensation for the loss of State Capital in 1976 and Egba wanted the new school in the City of Abeokuta, again, the Egba won the game which left the Ijebu gasping for oxygen.

How?

No one knew, but it was rumored that the new Head of State, General Obasanjo influenced the decision or he gave the order to the military Administrator.

No one could tell how the decision was reached and no one questioned a military government in those days. But the Egba got their wishes. It was a victory that made the Ijebu much more aggravated and bitter.

However, the Ijebu could not understand why Ogun State Polytechnic, the first and the highest institution in the State should be in the State capital and they prepared for the future. They frustrated the take-off of the project as files and documents for the project were dragged on or were delayed on the senior officers' tables in Civil Service until the Administrator had to physically show his might as the military Governor of the State.

Dr. Sonola, an Egba, was recruited from the University of Lagos to become the first Rector of the new school. He went through a lot of financial constraints from the unwilling State Civil Service as files were either delayed or misplaced to frustrate the takeoff of the Polytechnic.

The Polytechnic took off from the abandoned site of teachers college in Onikolobo and former site of Baptist Boys High

School at Oke Egunya with 220 students in January 1979 which was just a significant percentage from those sent away from Ibadan Polytechnic, the second batch came in six months later as the second set, they were joined by the those new students from the State meaning, the first and second set of the pioneer student of Ogun State Polytechnic were all admitted in 1979 with just six months separation for the National Diploma four year program.

Ogun State Government approved the 960 Hectares of rolling land bordered by Ogun River in the South for the permanent site of the institution with all the facilities similar to the university of Ibadan and Polytechnic.

The Rector, Dr. Sonola was given a difficult deputy from Ijebu precisely from Odo Pootu about ten miles to Ijebu Ode to manage the Polytechnic by the government. His duty was more of a spy, to slow down the progress or prepare to take over in case of the Rector's removal. It made the Rector to keep watching his back and it hindered his concentration on the development of the new institution.

When the country returned to civilian rule in October 1979 a former Ijebu Ode local government Chairman Chief Bisi Onabanjo became the elected Governor under the Unity Party Nigeria (UPN) a political party founded by the sage late Papa Awolowo, as a result all the past countable gains of the State capital were either reversed or slowed down.

Funding of the new Ogun State Polytechnic was drastically slowed down by the new civilian administration of Bisi Onabanjo and the students became involved in politics of the State.

Through the second year President Wassiu Popoola of the student union we approached Chief MKO Abiola to build a school Library because Governor Onabanjo did not believe in school libraries. Even if he did, the one in Abeokuta would not be of interest to him.

Ogun State Polytechnic was originally planned to have hostels like Ibadan Polytechnic for the students, it was supposed to extend its facilities to the bank of river Ogun, on the South end of the institution, Governor Bisi Onabanjo converted it to an off campus institution.

The students suffered on the uncared road to the school to attend lectures under unplanned and unreasonable environments. Perhaps the Governor's inability to have a University education could be responsible for his negative action against innocent students of the new institution.

As a journalist he should have known better, but his hatred blinded his reasoning power of fairness, to all the students that included those from his ethnic group, innocent students had nothing to do with politics except a conducive environment for knowledge, the Governor denied them that opportunities.

It was hectic attending lectures under the trees and in most cases in uncomfortable reading situations. We just wanted knowledge. We were happy our State had a Polytechnic we could call ours, which we hoped would compete with that of Ibadan or Yaba Tech in Lagos as we were motivated with words of encouragement from late Dr. Ajala the first Business Administration Head of Department, He died on the school campus after he mistakenly had medication from the ill equipped clinic on the campus.

"You will all be the future leaders of this State if you hang in there". He said.

He was right, 32 years after tears rolled down from my eyes as one of our 1983 set Senator Ibikunle Amosun became the Governor of Ogun State in 2011. I wish Dr. Ajala had been alive to witness that day. The memory of his words and encouragement kept us going;

President Barack Obama of the United States of America said, hope is not the ability to make it, but is that fire in you that keeps you going in the mist of difficulties, when you lose it, you are done.

The Students of Ogun Polytechnic kept hope alive in the core all the political problems from the government and society we found ourselves. Because of years of stagnancy in the admission policy in the old western Nigeria, the average graduation age for the first and second sets of Ogun Poly was 26-30 years.

When Bashorun MKO Abiola donated three hundred thousand naira to build the library we were very happy, but Governor Onabanjo did everything to frustrate the project; it wasn't until MKO Abiola resigned from the National Party of Nigeria in 1982 as the Chairman in Ogun State that his attitude to the library project changed.

It was a relief to Governor Bisi Onabanjo of the Unity Party of Nigeria who had a phobia for the political machinery of Chief MKO Abiola as the man who would destroy the control of Awolowo tradition in the western part of Nigeria.

Despite the fraternity of the NPN with Ogun Polytechnic Students Union the cooperation with MKO Abiola was different; he was a good man, who was always ready to help. He had the power, with all the three management polices of M's money, material and man to unseat any government. But he was constrained by the Yoruba solidarity for Chief Obafemi Awolowo.

Governor Bisi Onabanjo knew only Chief MKO Abiola had the potentials to dismantle the political empire of Chief Obafemi Awolowo with his newspapers. The National Concord first opened up the can of worms on the 350 plots of land at Maroko Lagos which was owned by DideOlu Estates owned by Awolowo family.

Chief Obafemi Awolowo and his family were the only shareholders. Chief MKO Abiola despite being one of the beneficiaries of the education scholarship policy of Chief Awolowo's government in the fifties he was bent on exposing the pretending socialist tendency of Awolowo as nothing but a cover up with capitalist tendencies of using the doctrine of social welfare to cover up and that was the foundation of the fears of Chief Bisi Onabanjo.

Governor Bisi Onabanjo came to Abeokuta for one purpose, to force complete control of Ijebu leadership on the State and he did just that without any respect for the feelings of others in the State or those of the minorities.

Governor Bisi Onabanjo established another Polytechnic at Ijebu Igbo at the same time the one in Abeokuta was operating from Onikolobo and Oke Egunya without or limited resources from the government.

Governor Bisi Onabanjo moved Dr. Femi Olubajo Deputy Rector of Ogun State Polytechnic at Abeokuta to the new Polytechnic at Ijebu Igbo without a clear cut or open competition for the position. It was a complete nepotism and disregard for decency or rule of law. If there was an interview for the position, a decision for his appointment had been pre-approved.

Also, his government established Ogun State University at Ago Iwoye which was a stone throw from his home town Ijebu Ode. He established Gateway Pharmaceutical at Ikangba Ijebu-Ode on the outskirt of his home town, if that was not enough; he constructed a bigger Market complex at Ita Oshugbo in the heart of Ijebu-Ode City, it made Oba Lipede market in the State capital to look like negligible quarters and all projects that could improve the economy were slated for the Ijebu Community.

Governor Bisi Onabanjo denied Abeokuta City's modern infrastructures; while roads and the drainage system in Ijebu Ode were constructed with the finest of modern concrete cement slabs and dualized carriage most of the roads were empty of any usage by motorists.

Sadly, the drainage systems of Abeokuta (the State capital) were made with ordinary nine inch blocks. Most of them could not withstand one raining season before they caved in. Somehow, in silence, the Egba, suffered under his Governorship.

Governor Bisi Onabanjo's detestation of the Egba or their heritage was so glaring; he tried to change the name of the State from Ogun to Gateway, as most projects were named Gateway instead of the name of the State. One could detect his revulsion for the word "Ogun" in all the projects he established.

To the Egba, Ogun River was and still is the heartbeat of the people. It was the River that prevented the Dahomey from invading Egba Kingdom in the era of slave trade. It was the river in which the history and heritage of the people was rapped: It's was like someone trying to change the name of your family while you are still alive, that was what Chief Bisi Onabanjo the man the press called Ayekooto did probably to slight the Egba for being too smart in getting the State Capital in 1976 since he was one of the groups that failed to approve Sagamu as the Capital when it was the in embryo in 1976. His policy as the governor was to make Abeokuta a State capital good only on administrative paper of the country.

As a former Chairman of Ijebu Ode's Local Government before he became the Governor of the State, he knew the politics of the State capital more than anyone. If the Ijebu had accepted Sagamu as the Capital, Abeokuta would not have taken it from the Ijebu province.

As expected, all these negativities upset the Alake of Egba land which resulted into open accusations on the legality of the government uneven distribution of projects by Alake of Egbaland Oba Oyebade Lipede.

At one time, Governor Bisi Onabanjo threatened to dethrone the Alake for questioning his authority as the Governor of the State but he was having similar problems with Awujale of Ijebuland Oba Sikiru Adetona over issues of his closeness to the National Party of Nigeria and Hon Bankole Okuwa a member of his party from Ijebu Ode for asking him to be fair to be all in the State he too was equally suspended from the party since his policies were breeding hatred in the State instead of love for all.

Surprisingly, in all these imbroglios, no one could say or point to any active role of Chief Obafemi Awolowo who kept his distance and never uttered a word to support or dispute the government of Onabanjo in Ogun State. He had his family roots in the two groups, his paternal side Ijebu, and maternal side in the Egba, Papa Awolowo relationship with Bisi Onabanjo went way back to all the political problems of the first Republic in the sixties.

However, Chief Bisi Onabanjo was not totally immoral to the Egba. He was a man who just believed in helping his own people first before others. His administration did most of the rural electrification in all the local government areas of the State, particularly, the neglected areas of Owode/Obafemi, IFO and Odeda local government. He established Gateway Hotels at Ijebu Ode, Abeokuta, and Sango Ota.

However, he saved the industrial take off of the State for his people. If the Egba hated his policies, it never affected the love they had for Papa Awolowo. They voted for the Unity Party of Nigeria despite the fact that Chief Odunjo an indigene of Abeokuta from Ibara of the Egba was the candidate of the opposition Party, the National Party of Nigeria and Bisi Onabanjo won the second term in 1983, however, the National Party of Nigeria in Ogun State without Chief MKO Abiola who had left the Party when his political future ran into a brick wall with the National Chairman of the Party Adisa Meredith Akinloye was left panting.

In fairness to Gov. Bisi Onabanjo the foundation of Egba Community's basic infrastructures could not match those of Ijebu community, it would amount to holding down the development of his people for others to catch up and it would be unfair to the Ijebu community itself.

Chief Sesan Soluade, a former French teacher at Lisabi Grammar School in Abeokuta in the seventies was Chief Bisi Onabanjo's deputy Governor. He was also a member of Lisabi Elites and a Chief in the palace of Alake of Egba.

The Deputy Governor was seen by Governor Bisi Onabanjo as more of an antagonist than a partner because of the Egba/Ijebu imbroglio. He was never really given a freehand as expected of a deputy in the civilian State government. He never had the respect of his people who expected him to challenge Onabanjo like the deputy Governor of Ondo State Chief Omoboriowo did. But "messieurs" which was the name his former students gave him in the days at Lisabi Grammar School, he played it cool with the ruthless Ijebu-man who operated with a pacemaker implanted in his heart, a thing the association of Ogun State students planned to remove from his chest when he denied us the Bursary award in 1980.

We did not know any better. Part of what became the foundation of the student unrest in the State when his government failed to honor his pledge to pay the five hundred naira Bursary award.

Chief Sesan Soluade was a complete gentleman. He loved to dress well. Whatever he wore looked good on him. His smile was infectious, but it was not enough to provide the missing leadership his people wanted from him to challenge the over imposing personality of Governor Bisi Onabanjo.

Gov. Bisi was indeed a proud man, but he looked down on the students Union or Ogun State Students National Association, when eight of us met with him in his office at Oke Ilewo to negotiate on the immediate payment of the Bursary.

Gov. Bisi Onabanjo in his wisdom or otherwise decided to lecture us of how to run our Association instead of honoring his pledge. He was not happy with the little allocation from the NPN controlled Federal Government to the State of Ogun.

President Sheu Shagari denied or limited his government financial support unlike other NPN controlled States. In the

Governor's eyes we were being teleguided by NPN in the State to disorganize his government which could be true because the President of the Student Union Popoola was too close to MKO Abiola, and years later he became the Representative for MKO Abiola London office.

Maybe the Governor was right but Wassiu Popoola had no influence on the National Association, his influence was limited to Ogun State Polytechnic, the national activities of the Ogun State students Association was strictly controlled by the President of the Association late Kehinde Sokeye who represented Ogun State Polytechnic and his inner group of membership from Yaba Tech, Universities of Ibadan and Ife respectively.

However, those of us from Ogun State Polytechnic were very considerate unlike the Students representatives from the University of Lagos and Ibadan. They had history of student unionism more than Ogun Poly with reputable Union leaders in the past like Banji Adegboro of Great UI in the seventies and Segun Okeowo of Unilag. They both had a better way of handling the situation in a more belligerent way than the layback method of Ogun Polytechnic led by my late friend Kehinde Sokeye as President of the national Association of Ogun State Student.

Kehinde Sokeye had ran for the office of President of Ogun Poly and lost to Wassiu Popoola of the Department of Accountancy in 1980 due to the internal problems of the Business Administration over his intention to run for the office of President.

At the time we wanted late Sola Alakija to run, at the end of the day, our camp was divided and Sola Alakija settled for the office of Welfare Secretary after a meeting with those of Popoola's group in the Accountancy Department.

The Presidency of Ogun State National Association was the only saving grace for Sokeye and how he could be compensated to keep the sanity of the fragile Union on the campus which the Polytechnic authority wanted to destroy, this writer who was known then as "Zik of Poly" and a member of the Editorial Board of the school new paper "the mirror" along with Kayode Awobadejo, and Makinde Ifedapo was the linking pin between the arrangement, until his death Kehinde Sokeye never stopped calling me "Zik of Poly".

Governor Bisi Onabanjo ran away from his office when the students came in thousands to his office at Oke Ilewo, the present site of OPIC, the Deputy Gov. Chief Sesan Soluade was almost beaten up; he was saved by this writer, because he was my former teacher at Lisabi Grammar School and my group respected the "Zik of Poly" when he asked them to spare his former French teacher. They did, but only, if the Deputy Governor could run away through the back exit like his boss. He did.

We took over the Governor's office, and had our President Kehinde Sokeye to sit on the Governor's chair for thirty minutes as the new Governor of the State.

All the chairs and tables in the governor's office were vandalized. Five bags of rice were found in the Corner office of the Confidential Secretary to the Governor. We opened it up and sprayed everywhere. We had fun vandalizing the governor's office.

In between the problems, the police probably acted on the order from above and never bothered us, until we arrested one of them in exchange for some students who were prevented from further damages.

Some of our students were charged to Ishabo Magistrate's court. It was funny to see the President of our Association the late Kehinde Sokeye in his blue suit with a big funny tie. I used to call it the National Bank tie, while he was holding briefs for the students, when he was not even a trained legal officer. Surprisingly, we won the case against Gov. Bisi Onabanjo in Magistrate Ashade's court.

The court castigated the Governor for making empty promises to the innocent students all over the country, a decision which made most of our parents to stop sending allowances to us because five hundred naira was a lot of money in those days.

Chief Dayo Abatan, who represented the Governor in the court, told this writer that he knew the NPN was behind the imbroglio and I could remember what I told him then. "If you guys would pay us our Bursary on time NPN would not be able to use us" He was quiet.

The following month, Governor Bisi Onabanjo paid the Bursary outstanding with a deduction for repairs on the damages to his office. That was the end of the Bursary award in Ogun State for a long time.

Gov. Bisi Onabanjo, never visited Ogun State Polytechnic or participated in any progress of the institution until Chief M K O Abiola left NPN and that was when the his government allowed the construction of Salau Abiola Memorial Library in honor of his late father. Salawu Abiola.

Seven Deadly Sins

Wealth without work
Pleasure without conscience
Science without humanity
Knowledge without character
Politics without principle
Commerce without morality
Worship without sacrifice.

— **Mahatma Gandhi**

3

MINORITY REPORT

So far, the first two chapters of this book tried to unveil the sources of the internal problems in Ogun State among the two major participants, Ijebu and Egba. It has left out the roles of the Awori, Remo and Egbado now called Yewa, the two major minorities in the State. What happened to them?

How did Ogun State Polytechnic the first higher Institution of learning in the State survive the policy of frustration and manipulation of Governor Bisi Onabanjo? Here are some of the questions raised by a few of my readers when my first article was published in the newspapers.

Some even wanted to know how Ogun Polytechnic moved from the Onikolobo and Oke Egunya campuses to the present Ojere campus site. Like the Oracle wrote on Facebook a social network site, Ogun State was indeed a bundle of intrigues and amazing revelations.

From history, Remo had a shared geographical link with both Egba and Ijebu. It was more like unwanted cousins to the two rivals. The major City of Sagamu was under the Akarigbo of Remo land, and could be traced to the same source from Ile Ife.

With the unfinished Yoruba wars after the collapse of Old Oyo Empire or the Kiriji wars over the control of route to Lagos or the Atlantic Ocean, every ethnic group within the Yoruba nation tried to change history to reflect its freedom and self-actualization.

After years of colonization by the British and partitions into provinces in which the Remo became one and under Ijebu, Remo became a problem for the Ijebu.

However, under the influence of the sage and undisputed Yoruba leader, the late Papa Awolowo, the loathing of the Ijebu for the Remo could never be openly expressed in public. Like I wrote before, Ogun State people enjoyed silent war strategies more than any Yoruba ethnic groups. Only those with "eyes and ears" could see or feel it.

Remo, like the cream of the Yoruba race, produced many professors, and administrators. They operate using the same doctrines as the Ijebu charity must begin at home then spread abroad. Their Yoruba dialect is more like the Ijebu than to the Egba. In as much as they claimed independence and separate identities from the Ijebu, the Egba treated them like the Ijebu.

The claim that everything above, the Niger River, East of Nigeria was Ibo, to the Yoruba, so it was, to the Egba parochial way of stereotyping issues in the seventies, Remo and Ijebu were the same but with historical shared territories. However, the Remo proved to be good friends and neighbors to the Egba but they always have to work harder to win the trust of the Egba, which was viewed with suspicions.

Furthermore, inter-marriages and business were not fully encouraged because of their closeness to the Ijebu or as a member of the old Ijebu province. They were indeed very genuine and sincere people which by commission or omission ended up in the Egba/Ijebu perpetual imbroglios.

The Ewekoro Cement Factory owned by West African Portland Company (WAPCO) was located between Wasimi and Papalanto villages (this writer's maternal historical birthplace) it was a pride to the Egba's contribution to the construction industry in Nigeria from the time of Western Region later under the Odua investment.

That was decades before Onabanjo became the Governor of the State. When the resource revealing committee discovered abundant limestone deposit in Ibeshe, Egbado now called Yewa land and Sagamu; Governor Bisi Onabanjo went for the project closer to

Ijebu than to Egba. Ibeshe was ten times bigger than Sagamu and it suffered neglect or was guilty by associate proximity to the Egba.

Most of the projects like Lapeleke Red Bricks and Ibese Cement were half-funded or abandoned. Funds and foreign partners were rushed to complete projects in Ijebu like Gateway Pharmaceuticals at Ikangba, Ijebu Ode and many more.

However, Remo benefited more than the Awori or Egbado now called Yewa under Governor Bisi Onabanjo. Probably because Remo was formerly part of Ijebu Ode Province or the secret unmentioned Awolowo factor.

The government located Ogun State teaching Hospital at Sagamu, a few miles away from Ikenne. The only separation between these two cities was the rubber plantation owned by the State Agricultural Development Corporation which was established by the old western Region.

Years later, Ogun State University was named after the late Governor Onabanjo and the Comprehensive High School Aiyetoro (established years before the creation of the State) became the only source of joy for the Awori people. It was made a satellite campus of the new State University.

Subsequently, apart from these higher institutions, the Egbado now called Yewa and Awori had no say in the State they found themselves.

Will they ask for their rights in years to come? Only time will tell.

They had no political heavy weights to ask these questions like Dr. Tunji Otegbeye and UPN Senate Leader late Senator Jonathan Odebiyi, the 1997 Senator, and late Afolabi Olabintan, were not interested in State politics because of other national pressing issues.

The battle for the survival of the Egbado now called Yewa and Awori within the State was left to the Egba as most of their cities remained undeveloped like the other Egba towns and villages.

Roads were un-tarred, hospitals were not built or funded and the water system had not improved from the time of the Old Western region under Chief Obafemi Awolowo, the past military governments of the western States of General Adeyinka Adebayo, Brigadier Oluwole Rotimi and Col. David Jemibewon respectively was not of help either.

The development in the State could be classified into two parts, a developed Ijebu Province (Ijebu/Remo) and the undeveloped province of Abeokuta comprising Egba, Egbado now called Yewa and Awori. That had been the policy from the time Chief Obafemi Awolowo was the premier of the Western Region.

Furthermore, all Ijebu and Remo towns had basic infrastructures years before other Yoruba towns, this meant the electricity, telephone and good roads network were functionally developed compared to the Abeokuta province of Egba/Egbado now called Yewa/Awori and all Governor Onabanjo did was to continue the domination as inherited from the time of Chief Obafemi Awolowo among the Yoruba tribe.

Sadly, as much as this writer respected the late Papa Awolowo for his leadership and foresight in most of the developments as the first Premier of the western Region and in Nigeria as a whole, that is the bitter truth of the foundation of the problems between the Egba and the Ijebu in Ogun State.

The assumption was that Papa Awolowo provided the Ijebu with a head start above other Yoruba cities. The problems of the Ijebu dominance were inherited by the new State and the late Governor Bisi Onabanjo allowed it by omission or commission to continue. He was ruthless with his tactics and strategies but

Awolowo was decent with his own version of *"sin of domination"* or relatively called *"the spine of control"*.

The "spine of control" of the late Obafemi Awolowo could not be noticed until the unit became a micro unit in the new State dispensation of Ogun until the merger of the two provinces as the new State in 1976 the Egba and other Yoruba restricted their social interaction with the Ijebu however the new State made it inevitable to interact or travel more within the State.

The merger opened the eyes of other ethnic groups as to their positions in developmental stages from the old Western Region to the new State specifically on the years unnoticeable of uneven distribution of infrastructures.

However despite the noticeable differences in Ijebu and Abeokuta provinces in terms of development inherited from years of following Awolowo and his politics, and uneven balances of projects in the two old provinces, it never destroyed the love of the ordinary people from Chief Obafemi Awolowo who had used his four cardinal programs with free education to cement the fraternity among the Yoruba race. And very few could see his policy of "Charity begins at home then spreads abroad" or the marginalization, which made Chief Sorunke a High Chief in Abeokuta to oppose Chief Awolowo at all levels but his people could not

Like the late President Ronald Reagan's doctrine of the "trickle down" theory in the United States of America, it would be hard to understand Awolowo and his policies.

By December 1983, three months after winning re-election, Governor Bisi Onabanjo was removed as the civilian Governor of the State along with all the civilian governors throughout the country.

A military coup announced General Mohamadu Buhari as the new military Head of State, the cigarette smoking President Sheu Shagari was placed under house arrest as well as all the other Governors of the 19 States in Nigeria.

It was alleged that the Federal Government under President Sheu Shagari was involved in a massive electoral fraud and manipulation of the government. His government was corrupt, marked with naked stealing from the public treasury and the ship of the nation was sinking, the military reported.

Somehow, the October 1983 election indicated the country was tired of the National Party of Nigeria as the ruling party. The result of the election was not the outcome of the votes of the electorates.

It was manipulated in favor of the National Party of Nigeria which claimed to have won the Governorship in Oyo, Lagos and Ondo States from the Unity party of Nigeria, however, those traditional States under the UPN were die-hard Awolowo based and it could not be true. It was like giving Texas in the United States of America to the Democrats in the Governorship elections in the nineties.

The numbers did not add up.

In most cases, the numbers of voters did not match the population in the State declared by the NPN influenced electoral body. It was a crude and untidy way to cheat in the elections.

The military coup d'état on the eve of December 31, 1983 which removed the civilian government was a welcome development to most Nigerians.

Surprisingly, the new government at the center announced Col. Oladipo Diya as the new Governor of the State in January 1984. However, Col Diya was another Ijebu from Odogbolu, about ten miles away from Ijebu Ode a City that was between the border of Ijebu and Remo land.

Gov. Diya changed the tempo of events on the activities of Ogun State government. He reversed some of the positive and negative policies of the former Governor. He cancelled the new Polytechnic at Ijebu Igbo and relocated all the satellite campuses of Ogun State University to Ago Iwoye the main Campus

Gov. Diya, an Ijebu man, never openly showed his love or support for the politics of division in the State. As a military officer, his orders were solely his or from Dodan Barrack Lagos, he had no open loyalty to anyone or the funny ethnic jingoism of Egba/Ijebu mentality. His kind of politics was different and the people of the State never understood his mission until he left office. But he actually reduced the debts of the State to only 28 million naira, a figure that would look like peanuts today. The State was saddled with a debt of 57 billion naira by Governor Gbenga Daniel in 2011 almost 28 years after.

Governor Diya's administration funded Ogun State Polytechnics at Abeokuta, and did many other projects which also increased the problems of the State. His actions in government were like a man without a people oriented mission. He had no respect for the feelings of the people and the traditional institutions.

The contention then was everything that Yoruba called "Omoluwabi" Governor Diya had none of them at all. He was just a soldier on a military assignment and only Dodan Barrack could check him.

If the people of Old Abeokuta province hated Governor Bisi Onabanjo at all, Military Governor Diya was a man the Egba and Awori hated with a passion. In his re-structuring policy, he sent a lot of people packing from the Civil Services and it affected a few members of Egba. For example, workers with the teaching and Civil Services were forced to retire, forced resignations or fired for flimsy excuses of not being able to recite the new National Anthem *"Arise oh Compatriot,* Nigeria call obey" as against the old anthem *"Nigeria we hail thee"* or the National Pledge, General Obasanjo forced on the people as military Head of State before he left office in 1979.

At one time in the life of his regime, reciting the national anthem and the pledge was almost the condition for promotion or picking up of paychecks, it was indeed a mental torture for the older people in the Civil Service.

The actions of the government in the State and others during the General Buhari government in Nigeria, was a gross violation of human rights and unfair labor practice, but the people of the State like every other State of the nation had no way of effecting a change, they suffered in silence.

The Military Governor then Col. Diya did not spare the Ijebu from his high handedness either. He came to clean the State that was his mission, but of what?

We never knew.

It was like the Egba and Ijebu called an arbitrator or Mike Tyson the boxing heavy weight Champion to settle a dispute between them,.

The above would be a better and realistic assessment of Governor Diya and his style of leadership. The people of the State were left panting from each pronouncement and the events from his office.

Diya, by his actions became the common foe and a monster as the Egba and Ijebu found a common ground to be friends for the first time in history of the State.

Col. Diya's action fell short of rational understanding of human behavior of Ranchos los Amigo theory, and he could be described as a man full of unstable and irrational decisions due to his military approach to issues that required a human touch.

When former Governor Bisi Onabanjo was jailed along with other Governors by the various tribunals on the order of General Buhari and his second in command General Tunde Idiagbon, various charges of corruption and nepotism, Nigerians witnessed a new system which made the civilian former Governors heroes in the minds of the people who enjoyed the freedom they had under civilian leadership.

The abuse on the rights of the people made all Nigerians to behave like the Israelites who asked Moses to take them back to Egypt after starvation in the desert.

All the people of Ogun State, including the Egba who were his political enemies wanted Gov. Bisi Onabanjo back more than they wanted to endure the unstable behavior of a military Governor like the rest of the country over the inhuman treatment by the military.

Governor Bisi Onabanjo and other State Governors of the country were found guilty by the military tribunal courts for abuse of office and embezzlement of public funds. He was accused of diverting the State's fund to his political party the UPN.

The jail sentences on all the formers governors in the country was funny, and beyond imaginations, some were sent to jail ranging from 25 to 125 years.

Some of them made the headlines like Gov. Jim Nwobodo of Anambra State who cried like a baby with a wet diaper and asked the Judge a funny question, he wanted to know, if the judge believed he would be able to genuinely serve all the 125 years because he was in his late forties.

Instead of condemnation, the people and the Press took side with the Oriaku as the Igbo people used to call eaters of people's wealth, and the tide changed for the military and it was the beginning of what led to the end of General Buhari's regime.

The health of Bisi Onabanjo or "Ayekooto" his pen name as an award winning journalist in the sixties became a concern to his friends and political associates. He was believed or alleged to be a man with Congestive Heart Failure CHF problems, saddled with unchecked pacemaker, he sometimes suffered shortness of breath, with swollen legs, because his heart was unable to provide sufficient pump actions to distribute blood flow to meet the needs of his body, because the military government would not allow him to travel out of the country for his annual medical checkup. He died shortly after his release from jail for diverting the funds of the State to the Unity Party of Nigeria.

However, the new Military Governor was horrible to observe at Ibara and Kuto roundabouts of Abeokuta City, with his green army suits, lots of soldiers and reckless driving on his way to the Ibara office and later to Oke Imosan. He made unscheduled stops and checked the schools and offices which often led to dismissals and loss of jobs for the good people of the State. Five minute lateness to work was enough grounds for dismissed from work.

This writer was then a teacher at Kobape High School a few miles away from Abeokuta. I saw how the Governor's entourage made infrequent stops as if he was chasing armed robbers; while in fact, he was chasing innocent workers with transportation problems at Ibara or Kuto who were probably late for work.

The people of the State lived in fear and missed Governor Bisi Onabanjo's soft cracking and feeble persuasive voice at least the "Ayekooto" as Bisi was also known by his admirers listened to us. One could hear the people talking in low tunes in small groups, they viewed Col. Diya as a man with an unstable personality, and all the news reports in the evenings of the State controlled media OGBC and OGTV were all about people losing their jobs or being sacked by the military Governor.

All the "Owambe parties" were cancelled or the people of the State were made to obtain special permits, before they had naming ceremonies or wake keeping parties in the State. What a strange development for our culture of waste and display of wealth and affluence on the people that loved parties!! Honestly, it could be likened to what happened in South Africa during the apartheid.

Also, Governor Diya relocated all the mechanic workshops from Abeokuta and major cities to places he called "mechanic villages" without any infrastructures, not even a public toilet.

Everyone was made to practice their trade in the dusty land of the so-called mechanic villages. Many of them had to walk five to ten miles to work. It was one of the greatest violations of human rights in the entire history of the good people of Ogun State.

The people of the State were all afraid to do anything. People were publicly caned by the soldiers for flimsy offences like crossing the road or being unable to recite the national pledge. It was the same treatment in all the States of the Federation as violation of human rights was seen as part of the military governance.

All the places of worship, the Churches, Mosques and traditional spiritual institutions were too afraid to pray or preach openly against the inhuman treatment from the military. If they did, it was the age of silent prayers and low profiles for all and sundries.

However, Diya's administration could be credited for the progress made with his environmental programs as most houses were forced to have toilets. Particularly in Abeokuta, and personal hygiene became one of the successes of his government.

Shokori stream and Ogun River were both closely monitored for abuse which was the practice for ages. Refuse collection was timely and the river and stream were both saved from inhuman treatment. If only Gov. Oladipo Diya had added a bit of a human touch to his actions maybe, he might have been more viewed positively, but he never did.

Furthermore, with no respect for the rule of law, many illegal appointments were made by Col Oladipo Diya. For instance, the appointment of a former, Rector of the abolished Ogun State Polytechnic at Ijebu Igbo Dr. Femi Olubajo as the General Manager of Gateway Pharmaceutical Company in Ikangba Ijebu Ode he became one of the reasons the joint project between Ogun State and Euro-Technical of Milano Italy died. Almost 50 million naira was lost at a time when the US dollar was almost at par with naira.

However, the appointment of Alhaji Rabiu as the General Manager of Ogun State's Agricultural Development Corporation from Agriculture Planning Department of the Ministry of Agriculture was one of the best in the State.

Alhaji Rabiu took the State agriculture to a new dimension with the improvement of the Ikenne rubber plantation, and palm produce at Apoje and Lomiro it became a model for the whole country.

"The smallest minority on earth is the individual. Those who deny individual rights cannot claim to be defenders of minorities."

-Ayn Rand

NEW LEADERSHIP

By August 1985, the country was fed up with the military government that removed President Sheu Shagari in December 1983. The gap toothed General

Ibrahim Babangida known as IBB or the evil genius had sent General Buhari packing as Nigeria's Head of State. He declared himself the first Military President of the Federal Republic of Nigeria. It was very unusual in the political history of Nigeria.

Colonel Diya who was promoted a Brigadier was also replaced with a man the Alake of Egbaland Oba Oyebade Lipede and the people of the State eventually loved with passion. The new military Governor of the State was Brigadier Dayo Popoola who was redeployed from Oyo State.

Gov. Popoola was a slim, good looking and tall military officer with a fine and polished character. He brought a new approach into the State. He never appeared threatening in any of his Statements. All his associates knew him to be firm and precise.

Despite records that showed he was from Ogbomosho in Oyo State, he spent his childhood in the City of Abeokuta. He was a humble man with respect for the people of the State.

He personally sent letters to all the indigenes of the State asking them to return home because the past Governor had instilled fear in the minds of the rich and poor. In fact, the rich stayed far away in Lagos and Ibadan to monitor the events of the State in the media from a comfortable distance, as many "Owambe" parties were suspended.

For the first time since 1976, there was calculated and cautious unity between the Egba and Ijebu. The military under former Governor Diya became their common foe. The new Governor also created comfortable platforms for harmony again in the State which was more than the previous administrations had done.

Governor Dayo Popoola demanded a new approach to the government, particularly from the divided State Civil Service. He demanded a new landscape development for the cities in the State; Abeokuta was experiencing uncontrollable expansion to the point of turning into a slum.

Furthermore, his government distributed amenities equally among groups of the State i.e., roads in Abeokuta City received attention from the government for the first time since 1976, also, he also planned the foundation of what became MKO Stadium in Abeokuta.

New dual carriage roads started springing up and Abeokuta started to look like a State capital to the discomfort of the perpetrators, that the City would only be a State capital on the administrative documents of the State.

All the amenities which the State capital was denied in the past were gradually coming into place, including all the statues of our past leaders as tourist attractions were encouraged by the peace loving Governor. That was until the military President General Babangida recalled him for another assignment in Lagos in 1986.

It was a sad day for the Egba, Awori, Remo and Egbado now called Yewa in Ogun State. Alake of Egbaland Oba Oyebade Lipede was close to the point of tears because Governor Popoola was a perfect "Omoluwabi". He came from a good home with respect for elders in which the traditional institutions were the general consensus of the people. He never allowed his military uniform or background to becloud his reasoning or to make him step on the toes of the elders in the State.

It was Gov. Popoola's behavior in the office of Governor that made the people of the State believe that in the Army, we had the good and the bad military officers. He represented the good and polished side of the Nigerian Army. Unlike others before him, he was the Governor who removed fears from his office which became a rally point for all; he was a good listener to all and sundries.

As the Project Secretary in Ogun State for one of the companies in the State, I had the opportunity to work very close with him on issues that affected Gateway Pharmaceutical Company at Ikangba Ijebu Ode.

One could recall the exact words of late Alake of Egba land Oba Oyebade Lipede in a sober tone when the Governor paid him a farewell visit along with the introduction of his successor Col. Raji Rasaki.

"How can the Military President Babangida give us a good man as Governor and at the time we were happy with him and his works and the love and unity he brought to the State, the military President IBB took him for another military assignment?"

The Alake of Egbaland Oba Oyebade Lipede lamented in his palace at Ake and he enjoined the successor Col Raji Alagbe Rasaki to act like Brigadier Popoola if he wanted to succeed.

General Popoola was probably the best Governor the State ever had and most of his legacies could be significantly noticeable in Abeokuta till today. His successor Colonel, Raji Rasaki from Ibadan was not literarily a tall man, a bit robust in the waist, and was a man always in hurry and his nose expanded whenever he was unhappy, very unpredictable, his ADC then was my friend now Colonel

Ademola Onalaja along with Col. Atanda who later became his ADC when he was transferred to Lagos.

However, the past records of Popoola served as a control on Raji Rasaki. If he had succeeded Governor Diya, his time would have been terrible. He lacked all the finesse and temperament of General Popoola.

General Popoola had in place, a foundation of solid checks and balances for future military Governors of the State, all which curbed Col. Raji Rasaki as a Governor who could have been worse than Brig. General Diya . Most of the time, the anger of this rascal could be seen from the way his nose expanded each time he was unhappy at some events in the State.

It was rumored that Governor Raji Alagbe Rasaki's mode or style of eating in the government house was different from that of Popoola, who ate meals in a very decent way unlike Raji Rasaki who approached his meal like a soldier on the battlefield and he often joked about it.

"Don't expect me to eat like Dayo Popoola put all the beef on the plate for me" he commanded his steward.

The new military Governor was not a man with polished English by Ogun State standards. He often butchered his sentences and the Nigerian Press had fun with most of his Statements. Like the unconfirmed story of the time he was commenting of a shoddy construction job done on a local bridge.

"Who built this gather," he said in the public, calling the bridge a gather, but this could not be confirmed or verified as the Governor was a graduate of top military institutions.

Sometimes, the Nigeria Press could be very mischievous, they created imaginary stories, they often added paparazzi and junk stories to discredit government officials, and all those stuffs they had with Governor Raji Rasaki and his typical Ibadan of Yoruba ascent could not help him either.

The Nigerian Press loved to make fun of the pronunciations of the Governor because of his special Ibadan ethnic ascent which was strange to the people of the State and he reminded them of the late Governor Barkin Zuwo of Kano State who could not understand the meaning of running mate in an election.

Barkin Zuwo a senator, thought a running mate was a co-contestant as against his vice or deputy for the office of Governor'. Or a politician in Oyo State Alhaji Adelakun who was asked to give his opinion on the constant student unrests in the country, the politician said, he did not think students were supposed to rest when they have books to read.

One could also recall when Governor Raji Rasaki visited the Gateway Pharmaceutical Company at Ikangba Ijebu Ode. The people thought he was going to sack the General Manager but he just walked away in disgust, the people were surprised when the Military President Ibrahim Babangida redeployed him to Lagos State as a military Governor.

The period under Raji Rasaki as Governor was almost a period of stagnation. He could not lay his hands on any new project. Perhaps one of his anti-corruption crusades was the way the Sole Administrator of Odeda's Local governments Mr. Fadulu was fired from the Civil Service for demanding a bribe from a contractor. He also disrespected the name and office of the Governor without knowing all his actions were on tape.

Navy Captain Mohammed Alabi Lawal succeeded Raji Rasaki as the Governor in December 1978, and by the time he left office he stole everything he could lay his hands on including carpets, rugs and government vehicles he had to leave in hurry. He started a Gateway line transport from Abeokuta to his home town Ilorin Kwara State. It was actually a conduit pipe to steal more from the government treasury as there was no economic justification for it.

Governor Lawal diverted the funds meant for the MKO Abiola dual carriage road at Abeokuta to his personal account and the road between Idi Aba to Asero were reduced to a single lane was against the dual carriage on the master plan.

When the people of Ogun State petitioned the presidency, the Nigerian leadership under IBB turned his eyes away from any investigation of Lawal. Later in life the people of Kwara State elected him as a civilian Governor of the State and the Oracle wrote three letters words to the people of Kwara State "Bless your Hearts".

Governor Lawal love for women was remarkable as most of the ladies in the Civil Service became his mistresses or overnight sleep partners, however, Lawal died in 2006 few years after he married his third wife, the press had accused him of laziness in his job as the governor of the State and as soon as he lost re-election in Kwara State due to the political machines of late Dr. Olusola Saraki, the godfather of the State political machines.

In between all these imbroglios and imperfect leadership in the State Ogun State never stopped being one of the best in the nation. The State had produced top educationists like Dr. Tai Solarin, world class Professors like Wole Soyinka, Mabogunje, Lambo, Soyode, Soyibo, Bamgbose, Olikoye Kuti, Soleye, Adesina and many authorities in medicine, laws, economics and other eggheads in various institutions.

What were the contributions of these great men to the State with the largest numbers of professors, doctors and lawyers in Nigeria?

If the people of Ogun State missed the democratic leadership of Bisi Onabanjo and level headedness of Governor Dayo Popoola, they were glad when the kleptomaniac Governor Lawal left the State. The Military Governor Oladeinde Joseph, who took over after him, was another character the State wished had never happened.

Perhaps the only regret Governor Lawal had was his inability to directly partake in the N100 million promised by General Babangida for the completion of the abandoned Gateway Pharmaceutical Company (GPC) at Ikangba, located in a suburb of Ijebu Ode, a few miles to Odogbolu the home town of General Oladipo Diya.

GPC was one of the most gigantic pharmaceutical companies in West Africa. It was conceived by the Unity Party of Nigeria under Governor Bisi Onabanjo. It was temporarily located at Abeokuta. Infact Governor meant it for Ijebu Ode but never told the people or the State Assembly before getting approval.

GPC was to manufacture and supply pharmaceuticals for a UPN controlled Federal government, if Chief Obafemi Awolowo had won the 1983 Presidential election, since he lost or the election was rigged in favor of President Sheu Shagari.

Ultimately, the GPC project became an elephant project for the Ogun State government the next question was how to reduce the six major pharmaceutical lines down to a manageable level that became a problem for the government and people of the State.

The lines of production when compared to the American owned foreign pharmaceutical company Pfizer in Lagos, was like comparing Mercedes Benz to a Volkswagen meaning, Gateway Pharmaceutical was the Mercedes Benz and Pfizer was the Volkswagen yet Pfizer was viable, GPC was not.

The foreign partner of the Project was Euro Technica of Milano, Italy. They had almost 30% of the shares which made Ogun State the majority owner.

Subsequent changes in leadership in the State and bad management; including Egba and Ijebu imbroglio destroyed the project that was meant to provide jobs to 500 university graduates and others, including suppliers and the possibility of yielding financial profits and opportunities to the City of Ijebu Ode and Ogun State as a whole. It was a sad situation.

The Ijebu felt cheated because of the location of Ogun State Polytechnic at Abeokuta in 1978, the Egba also felt a bigger project of this magnitude ought to be in the State capital. Both were greedy. None wanted to concede to each other in the distribution of any amenities or projects in the State.

Sadly, as it may sound, the State of Ogun was built on a cat and mouse relationship, suspicions and manipulation of ideas about the projects of any kind was evident. Just like the State Polytechnic, GPC became a victim of the same politics. None of the Egba or the Ijebu thought of the Aworis, Remo, Egun or Egbado now called Yewa, not even on the labor turn over and increasing numbers of unemployment of the youths coming out of the institution of higher learning from the State and the country, it was all about them.

What a people, what a society!

Gateway Pharmaceuticals however, from birth suffered lots of foot dragging policies from the State Civil Service. The first project officer was Alhaji Akingbala, an Egba, who started the project from the State Ministry of Commerce and Industries. He was responsible for the importation of all the materials and equipment to Ikangba from Lagos' sea ports.

However, his career was destroyed due to Egba/Ijebu internal problems. He thought he was being groomed to be the General Manager of the project but in reality he was not. By the time the government announced the appointment of an Ijebu man as General Manager, he knew his days in the company were numbered.

Alhaji Akingbala left the company and the State in shame as the new General Manager took firm control of the project, not for the goodness of the State, to participate in stealing materials like cables and equipment that would have completed the project on time without the support of the Federal Government.

This author knew Alhaji Akingbala from his cousin's circle of friends Adejare Shoyoye fondly called Pappy Jay, but he did not know in future, he would take over his job as the Project Secretary of GPC.

Part of Akingbala's job was to "take care" of the Customs officials at the corruption infested Tin Can Island Lagos before materials were released by clearing and forwarding agents at the sea and airports as approved by management verbally. See to the importation and delivery of materials to the site at Ikangba a suburb of Ijebu Ode on Obalende/ Odogbolu road.

"Take care of the Customs" in those days meant "bribe", "grease" the palm or "settle" the system, in any way possible, to get things done from Lagos. He did exactly what he was asked to do, but he never obtained the order for his action in writing, and that was what used to get him out of the system.

When you graduated from school in those days, you inform cousins, relatives and other family members of your employment intentions. After you have sent several applications to many companies, you would wait for any invitation for an interview and as soon as one came, you would start to press the button on who could influence your appointment.

That was the practice in those days. It was not about the quality of your grade in school, it was who you knew. Those with first-class grades ended up getting only teaching jobs while those with ordinary grades got better jobs in the banks and oil companies.

I had no support from family members to lean on apart from my sister; I had no one to turn to. My favorite cousin Pappy Jay was also teaching at the Polytechnic, after returning from the United States of America with chains of academic degrees.

After doing a lot of job searching and facing disappointments, he eventually settled down for a teaching job at Ogun State Polytechnic at Abeokuta.

My uncle on the paternal side, Chief Kotoye, was also having problems with his partners at Societe Generalle Bank, over board control of the shares which late Chief Dr. Olusola Saraki left behind when he moved on to join the National Party of Nigeria as the Senate Majority leader.

Chief Kotoye claimed his friend Dr. Saraki used his name as collateral security to borrow lots of money from the Bank to run for the office as a Senator under the National Party of Nigeria which he won and until the funds or loan was paid back, it would be difficult to return the shares to Dr. Saraki. Those were the words of Chief Kotoye when I asked him for details from his office at Ikoyi in Lagos.

The legal tussle between Kotoye and Saraki became national news on the pages of Nigeria news media. The Press took side with Dr. Olusola Saraki and Chief Kotoye on the pages of the newspapers and in the public opinion was found guilty, when the fact of the case was yet to be concluded by the court.

In-between, one of the French managers of the Bank that flew in from France to testify in support of Chief Kotoye was killed in Lagos before he could make his court appearance and his other partners ran back to France, as a result of these problems, Chief Kotoye was not in the position to help a family member.

After several visitations to his office in Lagos and his brother at Abeokuta, I gave up on him.

The future was just how we had to fend for ourselves and teaching was still the only place that offered an opportunity for those without financial backing, and that was my situation like most of my colleagues when we graduated with a Higher National Diploma from Ogun State Polytechnic in 1983.

However, as fate would have it, one of my distant Uncles on my paternal side was transferred from Ilorin in Kwara State to Abeokuta. Uncle Ayo Obaseki was an engineer who became the Director of the Energy Distribution of Nigeria Electric Power Agency (NEPA) His father was from Benin City in Edo State, and we favored each other a lot. He was slim, a fast talker and had no patience at all. Those are also my traits.

Uncle Ayo Obaseki introduced me to the State Commissioner of Ogun State Ministry of Finance, who was his golf playing Buddy and his support for the State government in the rural electrification projects. In the past, he was seen more from a professional angle an outsider. It became visible to the government that they infact had a person from the State on his mother's side as the Director of the Federal Energy system in the State.

They needed him and I became the bait to get him to do more for the State.

The Commissioner of Finance in his office offered me the options of working with Towergate Insurance or Gateway Pharmaceuticals: I took the GPC option and my job was the project Secretary because the job requirement included banking experience which I had from National Bank of Nigeria in the seventies unknown to the Commissioner of Finance I had applied several times without any response from the same company before due to ethnic politics.

However, I believe that without my uncle's help under normal circumstances, I was qualified for the job but the system would never have allowed me to get the job on my own merit.

You have to know someone!

My job was to establish liaison connections with the Central Bank of Nigeria and the Federal Ministry of Finance and contend for the release and renewal of Form "M" and other government agencies. I had to attend meetings as Secretary for the project with the State Department of works and Housing along with technical partners Euro Technica from Italy.

The politics of the State were deeply embedded in the company. Just after the General Manager got rid of Alhaji Akingbala and I came on board I sensed the problems I could find myself in, as traps were set for me to fail like the previous project Secretary.

The same principle of "take care" of the Customs when we needed to clear goods at the Tin Can Island Ports was extended to me just as it was for my predecessor.

As a former bank official I knew better I wanted things in writing. When given verbal instructions to carry out by the management I would immediately write a memo, and asked whoever gave the verbal instructions to confirm it in writing before I proceeded.

That became a problem for the management but I was not ready to become a victim like the previous manager. In business school we were told it is called CYA *"cover your ass"*

The new Egba on the job as project Secretary was different from the last victim. I was a fast learner and my boss was difficult because he intended to fill the position with an Ijebu man and I could not afford to fall into the trap.

I reported my problems to the supervising Commissioner of Commerce, the late Mr. Sunday Edun, who summoned both of us into his office and warned him to change his attitude or be fired. Instead of cooperation, the stage for open resentment was set between us and I decided to acquaint myself more with political leaders of the Egba to protect myself.

Uncle Obaseki, who introduced me to the job, could not believe some of the stories I told him. To him my boss was a good guy, and I must have been the bad person.

He never really knew me as a kid and he believed the Dr. Femi Olubajo, the General Manager more than he believed me, he belonged to those careless and unsuspecting Egba who went to school outside Abeokuta without understanding the behind the scene wars in the State, the policy of manipulation was strange to him, until I brought home the official files for him to read. It was then that he realized the General Manager was setting me up to be jailed or be fired like he did to Alhaji Akingbala.

The revelation of the negative behavior of my boss to my uncle earned me his respect. He saw how diligent and completely devoted to my job I was, but my interests had changed. I was more interested in getting more education than getting involved in the internal politics of the State and company. I planned my exit.

In October 1987, I became the first Ogun State Polytechnic Student along with Mrs. Obe to be admitted to the University of Ibadan for a Master's degree in Business Administration.

As soon as I applied to the Board through the General Manager for a study leave with pay, Dr. Olubajo denied the request. Infact, he asked the Board to alter my application from study with pay to resignation. This was to enable him to hire someone, without the approval of the Board Dr. Femi Olubajo was already shopping for a replacement.

The Board of Directors under the Chairmanship of Professor Bamgbose asked Dr Olubajo to submit three names for consideration as my replacement at the next meeting and he did.

They were all Ijebu names; the Board rejected his proposal and approved my study leave without pay and a promise to keep my job after 18 months of school which was the bipartisan way for him to save his dignity. I obtained the approval in writing as a future tool against any misrepresentation of material fact. It was the smart thing to do.

Every attempt by another member of the Board, Mr. Bankole, and an Egba man, to place me on half pay and the suggestion that the company pay my tuition was vigorously rejected by the management.

However, I had the support of my landlord, late Engineer Yomi Adenekan who was like a brother to me and my family. We knew it was going to be tough, but if I needed to make progress I would have to do just as I planned. I remembered the advice I gave to one of my students when I was a teacher at Kobape High School a few miles away from Abeokuta in 1984.

As the class progressed, and I was enjoying the intellectual nutrition I was giving my students, one of them raised his right hand and he asked the question that changed the lives of everyone in the classroom.

"Sir, how will I know if I will end my life as a poor man?" He said.

Tunde was the first son of his polygamous father to attend High School in his village. His mother a sugar cane seller had taken a gamble on him, that a brighter future would be his if he could make it through academic pursuit. Unlike his other brothers who were mechanics, vulgarizers and taxi drivers.

It was not a question for the economics, commerce or the accounting subjects I was assigned to teach in the school. It was a question out of curiosity, self-help, self-development and mentally challenging from a teenager of only 15 years old in the small village of Kobape in 1984.

I walked away from the blackboard, and looked at him directly in the eyes and I knew my answer would not only be for him, but everyone including me his teacher.

Secretly, in my heart, I prayed to God, "Let me be able to communicate in a way that I will be an agent of change for my students."

"Do nothing while others are. When people are reading-don't, when they are positively investing in education, do nothing. When they are working or looking for jobs, do nothing. When your mates are putting their lives together, do nothing. Just fold your hands and watch the events of life like a parade." I said.

I stretched my hands out like a pastor facing a congregation I looked directly at them, about 40 students in my Commerce class, innocent kids unsure of the future and said in a very emotional voice you can't imagine what it's to feel like a Pentecostal pastor looking for souls to win for Jesus Christ.

"Remember today in your lives. If you have to cross the Rubicon of poverty in this most difficult period of your life, my dear students please invest in your life like a new product. Pray and talk to God to help you out, and do the best you can at all time.

"Remember when you stop trying, you stop being number one and then you have the answer to your questions."

"I hope I have answered your question!!" I said.

Perhaps it was too deep for my students because the class was silent. But I knew, I had said the right words, I have never stopped thanking God for that day. Most of my students at Kobape High school became top Chartered Accountants and Business executives. They took my advice seriously and ran away with it. I was glad God spoke to them through me.

Equally, I was happy that Tunde asked the question. I have never stopped challenging myself and the day my eyes are closed finally, will be the day of self-actualization for me.

I disagreed with Abraham Maslow on his theory of hierarchy of needs and self-actualization process because the end of one goal to me is the beginning of another.

No one can reach the point of self-actualization - that is my belief.

My years at the University of Ibadan were tough, but I was very determined. I gave my best at all times to my studies; I was comfortable with my studies, and other people on the campus.

I was back in the City of my birth Ibadan. The air was friendly and familiar. It was like going back home again and remembering all my childhood pranks at Ekotedo where it all began for me which made me wonder why Abeokuta could not think or act like the people of Ibadan. Nothing matters except humor and a society without gobble of manipulation or frustration.

The University of Ibadan campus reminded me of my days as a Binding Clerk at the National Achieves in the seventies. It was our joy even though; we were not students of the university in the early seventies. I along with Sunday Odutola, Tunde Lawal, Francis Osifoh, Dan Imokhome or Garba, Edigan Ailoje, Oke, Ogun, Stella Odua, Olu Ukwu, Bose Asekome and other staffers of National Achieves located in the Aberdina area the University of Ibadan, we were able to get the subsidized meals from the cafeteria or visit friends at the students residential Halls. We prayed one day that we too, would be there as students.

The Citadel of knowledge was built like a typical British University, very conducive for academic facilities, recreational environment, spiritual linages for all faiths, including atmospheres of seriousness and carelessness, the right to succeed or fail was entirely up to the student.

Ogun State Polytechnic at Abeokuta functioned as an off-campus system. I longed for a University community environment like that of the great University of Ibadan. I enjoyed every minute of it.

The University provided the much missed goals in my academic pursuit. The University Library became my favorite place on the campus, not only because I love to read but I had no money to play around with. I took my frustrations out on my books, and I read voraciously.

Moreover, studying at the University of Ibadan had preoccupied my dreams from the day I visited Mr. Austin Ugbuegbu, who was my High School Mathematics teacher. He became a post graduate student in Econometrics in 1974. He had taken me around the campus, and said, he knew, one day, I would be there as a student from the glitter in my eyes.

He was right. Except that it took 13 years for that prediction to come true.

Professor Fafunso of the Biochemistry department, provided me with a room in the boy's quarters of his official quarters, he was a friend of my Ekotedo brother, Justice Deinde Soremi. He was then the Director of Public Prosecution DPP in Ogun State Ministry of Justice, along with Justice Demola Bakre who also grew up with us as a senior brother from the days at Ekotedo, the both of them used to address my father as senior that was the custom based on age as it was the yardstick in those days.

Justice Soremi was also one of my advisers who helped to avoid some of the General Manager's various traps. Brother Deinde, (as I used to call him) was a very friendly senior, one could see his love and affection from the way he took care of our interests by listening to us and our problems.

He was more like the older brother I never had. I could tell him everything; I mean anything from women, money, social or family problems and his advice never failed.

When he became a Judge and friends started addressing him as "My Lord" I was confused on how to address him, when I called him "Brother Deinde", his friends tried to correct me. In those days, he told me I should address him in any way I was comfortable with, because he would always remain a brother to me first, no matter what his position. He was right, that was his place in my heart, a brother before anything else.

In the same way, I was close to Justice Soremi; I was with Dr. Fafunso as well. He introduced me to the Executive Director of Pfizer for the three months internship with the Marketing Department of the Pfizer Pharmaceutical Products at Ikeja in Lagos where I worked directly with Sam Ohambuwa with Mr. Ajibade both were the brains behind the marketing and sales department of Pfizer Products limited in Lagos.

The MBA program went faster than I expected and when I was "broke" or short of funds I converted my Volkswagen Beetle into a taxi cab or "Kabu Kabu" from Abeokuta to Ibadan and along with my little savings and the support of friends plus the grace of God; I was able to go through the 18 month MBA programs on time.

Most of the workers from Pfizer Pharmaceutical Products in Lagos were friendly, those who were indigenes of the State were impressed with the GPC project in Ogun, you bet, and I was a good advocate of the largest pharmaceutical company in the State. Together we visited the site and all of them wanted to help.

I remember in particular that, Mr. Ajibade who was the Marketing Director and most of them were minorities in the State or Egba and the politics of the State did not favor their contributions.

I also recall after the Board of Directors of Gateway Pharmaceuticals approved my study leave without pay, Dr. Femi Olubajo, the General Manager called me into his office for a meeting. He advised me to change the 18 months study leave without pay to 30 months because the University was set up differently from that of Ogun State Polytechnic, and the dreams of completing the program on time might not be easy as I thought.

I knew he stood between me and the study leave, so I did not consider his advice genuine. I looked him directly in the eyes and said, if the program was reduced to six months, instead of eighteen months, that would be the time for me to complete it.

I never failed any of the classes, although I could have done better if I had all the money and resources my colleagues had.

I did make new friends at the University, who were mostly from my department: Dr. Mohammed Santuraki, who later became the Managing Director of Nigeria Agricultural Bank, he was a very brilliant Hausa man and a veterinarian before he became part of the

MBA program. We talked on all issues, politics religion and the stereotype idea of both tribes; by the time he left he changed the views of most of us from the South. What a great guy!

Ralph Osayemeh the author of "Principles of Banking" who became the Managing Director of Commerce Bank and was President of Nigeria Bankers Association, was then Assistant general Manager Personnel for UBA, Tunji Latinwo was Managing Director of Imani Mortgage bank in Lagos, Dr. Ilesanmi, Omidiji and Lemmy Omoyinmi was President of Yaba Tech Student Union. They all came with the full backing and resources of their organizations, which I never had except for my determination.

I could not socialize the way I wanted because I was an indigent student. *You need money to buy Whiskey* like they say in Texas'. You needed money to enjoy the MBA programs in those days and my fiscal cliff affected my life style in the school I never stopped blaming the management of my company GPC for their refusal of my study leave with pay, like most of my colleagues.

Some of my colleagues were lodged in hotels and they had the best of everything to support them in the program. I didn't have that kind of support and as a result my rent was suspended until I could come back as promised by my landlord, but that was okay, no one told me it was going to be easy, it was a task I knew I had to finish.

I graduated on time and I did not repeat any of my classes. But the strain of it left me bitter about the system. I was even contemplating a law degree after the MBA but the University system in those days considered me more like a career student; their thought was give others a chance to attain a university degree like you did. The university admission was keen and rigid many were on the waiting list.

Dr. Patrick Oribabor who came on sabbatical from the University of Ife or Obafemi Awolowo University, for a year's teaching program, we became friends and he wanted me to pursue a post-graduate degree in the University of Ife. I turned it down because I was interested in returning to my job at Ogun State. I also wanted to finish up GPC projects a decision I believe was an error of judgment on my part.

By the time I returned to GPC at Ijebu Ode, it was a sorry situation. The whole place had been vandalized and stealing was done openly and without fear as the police and the management of the company were actively involved.

It took a phone call from the Alake of Egbaland Oba Oyebade Lipede to the Governor before I could even return to my seat, as management wanted me out of the system.

Power can be very interesting if it flows from the right source. The State supervising ministry for GPC the project Ministry of Commerce, on the order of the State Governor, took me directly to the site at Ikangba with OGSG air-conditioned 504 SR with a letter for immediate re-absorption.

In those days, a Peugeot 504 SR with air-conditioning made some humming sounds that usually announced the arrival of the government official. The atmosphere was stressed, the driver took the instruction from the Commissioner of Commerce straight to the General Manager's office, that the office must be opened and cleaned before Mr. Sowunmi could come out of the humming air-conditioned government OGSG car.

The General Manager had converted my office into a file room and had told the staff Mr. Sowunmi would not be coming back because he knew; I was popular with the staff. But that day he was forced to eat up his words; he got the office cleaned in the presence of the staff from the government office of Abeokuta.

I sat quietly in the back seat of the car while my office was being cleaned. I was thinking of everything I realized I was no longer representing myself, I was there as one of the pillars of the State politics, to help, to build, and to finish the project and to lift up the workers.

It was my mission, and that was what I did, I called the staff meeting and looked into all the denied benefits of the junior staff, unpaid overtime of drivers and workers, and recommended immediate payment of all the denied benefits.

It made the General Manager very uncomfortable.

Ijebu Ode Central Mosque.

Ojude Oba Festival Ijebu Ode

Ojude Oba Celebration very popular with the Ijebu

Lisabi Festival in Egba nation

Ayo competition winner during the Lisabi Festival

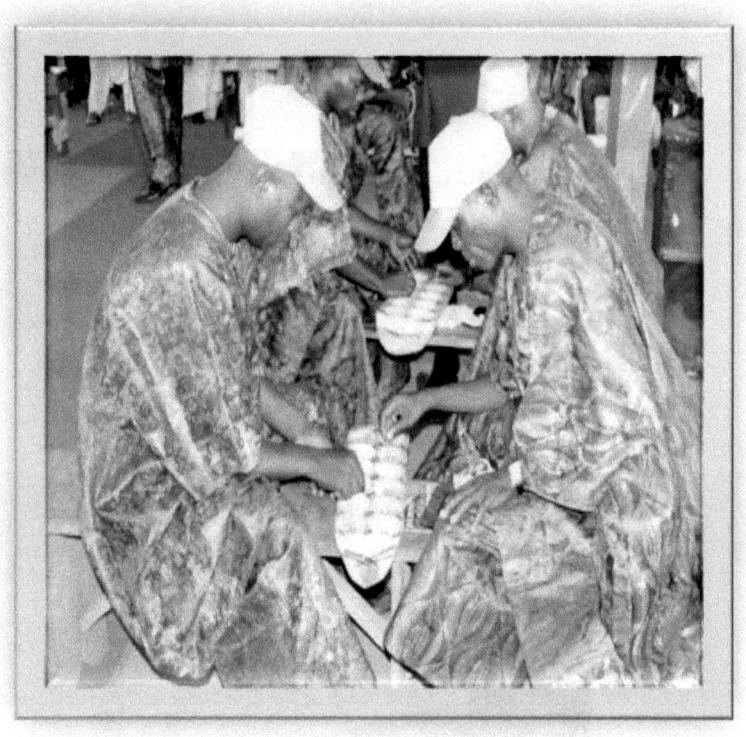

Ayo Opon a very popular tradition game among the Yoruba

Almost 99 years after Abeokuta had the first electricity in 1914in Nigeria, Ogun State Govt under Ibikunle Amosun commissioned the first Abeokuta overhead Bridge in 2013 it attracted lots of people on the day it was commissioned.

"The rights of every man are diminished when the rights of one man are threatened."

— John F. Kennedy

WHY the GPC BOARD WAS DISSOLVED?

The previous Board of Directors of the Gateway Pharmaceutical Company under Professor Bamgbose of the University of Lagos Teaching Hospital was dissolved. It was replaced with the cabinet members of the new military Governor Lawal to facilitate his program and intentions.

Whatever the reasons for the dissolution of the Board of Directors, it didn't appear to be in the best interests of the State.

Professor Bamgbose was a born again Christian, from the minority town of Igbesa. He was a Professor of Medicine from the University of Lagos Teaching Hospital (LUTH). He was appointed Chairman of the Board of Directors for the company by the previous military Governor, Oladipo Diya.

Professor Bamgbose was a professional colleague of Professor Olikoye Kuti at the University Lagos Teaching Hospital (LUTH).

The Minister of Health, visited the site along with military President Ibrahim Babangida and after the usual military inspection of the factory without the approval of the Supreme Military Council, He asked the General Manager, how much it would be needed to complete the project.

The General Manager without consulting the Project Secretary, who was this writer, or the Accountant, or the Board of Directors, gave a N100 million figure on impulse. There, on the spot, a Presidential promise of 100 million naira was given for the completion of the project. The Board of Directors was to act in league with the Federal Ministry of Health in Abuja for the release of the fund.

Governor Lawal could not believe the unexpected windfall and approval of N100 million by General Babangida and he did what most thieves would do.

Since it would be difficult to influence the "born again" Chairman of the Board of Directors into sharing what appeared to be "manna" from Abuja, the Governor dissolved the Board of the company and appointed his kitchen cabinet of commissioners as members of the new Board then waited for the loot to come.

However, he was wrong! Professors Bamgbose and Kuti were both professional colleagues from the University of Lagos Teaching Hospital in the Faculty of Medicine LUTH. It was agreed in the presence of this writer who was then on study leave (although never stopped visiting the former Chairman Professor Bamgbose who suffered a stroke and was paralyzed on his upper right extremities.)

We agreed to impress on the Federal military government to release the funds gradually to the new Board of the company, along with monthly performance reports on the project.

By the time Governor Alabi Lawal began thinking and dreaming of the millions of naira from Abuja, he was out of State for another military assignment. He left the "manna" project to the new Governors Navy Officer Joseph.

Based on the discussions with the Federal Minister of Health, somehow only N40 million was released out of the N100 million promised by the Federal Government with a progress note attached.

Regrettably, out of N40 million, only N5 million was actually spent on the project. The rest of the 35 million naira (out of greed) was shared by those at the top excluding the Accountant of the company.

When a crime of looting is done without the active knowledge of the Accountant in any organization, the tendency for it to be exposed in future could not be unexpected. The Accountant of GPC was not carried along. He decided to sing like a canary Bird.

This author had resigned from the services of the company and took another private sector assignment in Lagos six months before the release of funds from the Federal Government of Nigeria. Was the Accountant cheated? Why was he left out of the loop? The answer will be revealed in the next chapters.

"A nation of sheep will beget a government of wolves."

— Edward R. Murrow

6

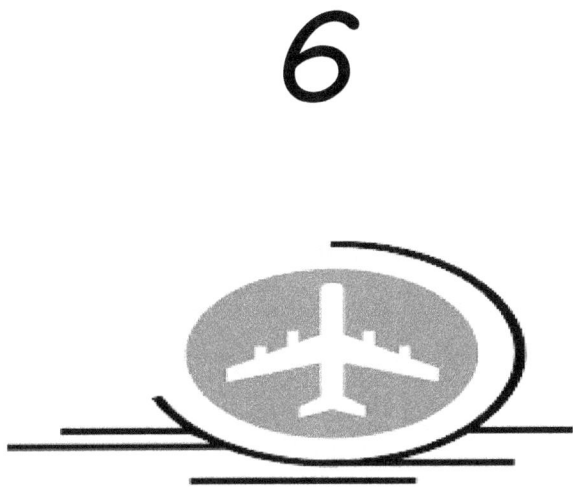

WITHIN

He Gateway Pharmaceutical Company was like an epileptic child from inception. It never recovered from the open and naked stealing by those government officials involved or all the parties involved, everyone wanted what they could get from the company.

The General Manager of the company was promoted to the position of Managing Director on a project that was still under construction. Based on his Statement to the State Board of inquiry years later and that was when Col Akintonde became the military Governor or Administrator of the State, which was the situation before Governor Osoba became the new Civilian Governor under the Social Democratic Party (SDP) in 1992.

The Egba for the first time had their own man, Chief Olusegun Osoba as the new Governor of the State. He was a newspaper guru like the footsteps of late Governor Bisi Onabanjo. He made his career at the Daily Times of Nigeria as Managing Director and other newspapers like the defunct Daily Sketch at Ibadan in Oyo State.

Chief Osoba was one of the beneficiaries of Chief Ajose's legacy of inner development in the private sector. He was prudent and diligent news reporting staff person for the most powerful Daily Times in the sixties and seventies, some of his most remarkable overages were the events of the first and second coup, the civil war and many other significant and bold news reporting episodes made him exceptional. He met the prerequisite of Chief Ajose the doyen of Nigeria Press for his policy of internal sourcing for future leaders of the newspaper.

As a friend of the military officers from many generations, Governor Osoba once said:

"The best way to move up in life is for a man to know how to mix friendship with loyalty,"

Whatever it was, it actually helped the man who took more chieftaincy titles as "Aremo" of most of the cities in the State than doing the job of governance. However, he was too close to the Ijebu to the discomfort of the Egba. At one time the Egba thought Governor Osoba was not an Egba. His family tree in the Oba area of Egbaland could not be traced by those mischievously searching anything.

No matter how small, they tried to pull him down politically, however, they were wrong as Chief Olusegun Osoba's action was no different from any Egba in government, neither nepotism or favoritism was fair nor balanced, but politics was more than the doctrine of fair balanced.

Governor Osoba's administration by simple nepotism tendencies of the past ended as a disappointment to the Egba and the people of Obafemi Owode the local government of his hometown. His people thought Osoba would modernize their primitive locality to the same level of the Ijebu towns, or those in Lagos State. But history again repeated itself like it did in the seventies when the Egba were disappointed with Governor Oluwole Rotimi of the old western State.

Historically, when Governor Adeyinka Adebayo left as the Governor of Western State he was replaced by Brigadier Oluwole Rotimi in 1972. The Egba were happy with the visible extended development General Adebayo did with the Ekiti from, Aramoko, Igede, Ikoro, Iyin, to Ado Ekiti and the location of government projects and factories in Ekiti province would be similarly done in the Abeokuta province, the Egba thought.

General Oluwole proved them wrong, he made it known, and he was going to be the Governor for whole of Western State not just for the Egba, unlike the selfish interests of the previous administration. What could be closer to his influence on the lives of his people was the location of the Wire and Cable industry along Ibadan and Abeokuta Road.

The project was still in Ibadan nothing of significant could be pointed to as the Egba were disappointed in his leadership, which despite the so-called western education and closeness to civilization before any ethnic group in Nigeria or Yoruba nation had no significant project or factories other than Top Brewery owned by Chief Lawson, Gov. Oluwole Rotimi was never forgiven by his people, that was in 1972.

Almost 20 years after, this incident they felt let down and the misunderstood *"Aremo of every City"* in the State. All Gov. Segun Osoba wanted was traditional titles, instead of proper management of the State that would have uplifted his people.

However his term was cut short by General Sanni Abacha who dissolved the civilian government after the failed 1993 transition government was set up by General Ibrahim Babangida before he left office.

Sadly, the Egba could not point to anything of importance from Governor Osoba in his first term in office the roads still remained primitively constructed. Hospitals and basic infrastructures denied by the past administrations were not corrected; it was very disappointing for the Egba or the Yewa.

Unlike Bisi Onabanjo, his government was a big failure in the opinion of his people. He approved the construction of third bridge on the Ogun River that turned out to be too narrow for 21st Century imaginations, and it was supposed to link up the Adigbe area of the City, Gov. Osoba's so called Ota Water project opened with pump and pageantry and dried a few days later.

However, the petition from the accountant Olusegun Olusoga on the shared Gateway Pharmaceuticals Company fund from the Federal government reached Governor Osoba's desk before he left office and he did nothing.

First of all, he was too close to the military. Secondly, he had his own agenda. What was his agenda? Was it in the interest of the State?

What happened to the Accountant who wrote the petition?

"One of the penalties of refusing to participate in politics is that you end up being governed by your inferiors."

- Plato

"...........................This project will need to be reviewed with a new management, from the looks of things it will take five years to get to this level. As a man in a hurry with a post-graduate degree in Business from the University if Ibadan, I do not see myself hanging around on a project that too many forces are planning to kill on a daily basis. I have attached a short note on plans of action to be taken by the government If and when we have a serious-minded Governor who loves the people and this project. When the plans are executed as intended, within six months GPC products will hit the pharmaceutical market in Nigeria and indeed West Africa............................."

7

THE NEXT STEP

T

He overleaf was an extract from my letter of resignation to management and the Board of Gateway Pharmaceutical Company before I bowed out in 1989. I never stopped wondering if Ogun State would one day do the right thing; hopefully stay with the truth and love of the people.

It was sad to walk away from a project that my MBA thesis and three months understudy of activities of Pfizer products in Lagos was based on. But to stay meant I would have to join them or lose my life. I decided to walk away from it.

It was sad, but it was indeed the right decision for me and my family. The events that happened after I left made me to appreciate the coherent actions of my decision.

As a result of the petition from the Accountant on the project, the new civilian Governor Olusegun Osoba had a meeting with the Managing Director to request details on the mismanagement of the Federal grant of almost 40 million naira on the Gateway Pharmaceutical Company. Bu when he heard the details of all the military people who were involved, Governor Osoba failed to uphold his oath of office for justice in the State and advised the Managing Director to take care of the Accountant.

Whatever that meant, it was something to investigate in the future. It could have meant to give the Accountant something to keep him quiet by simple imagination, but it turned out to be something else.

The Managing Director was armed with the misunderstood words from the Governors "take care of the Accountant." He requested the Accountant to present for review his detailed qualifications and credentials for the position were holding as the Chief Accountant of the company.

He was then told that he would be going on a study program. The same way, the late President Yar'Adua sent the first Chief of EFCC Nuhu Ribadu for a course at Kuru. He later turned around and demoted him before he was eventually sacked from the position.

It was an identical script here. Sometimes you wondered if the Nigerian political chess players received their scripts of actions from the same source.

The Accountant was a graduate with a Higher National Diploma who finished with a barely passing grade, or what those in schools we called *"let my people go."* He was one of the first sets graduates from Ogun State Polytechnics in 1982, and he had no

ICAN certification like a CPA but after several years in public service as a finance officer he became competent in the job.

He could not produce the ICAN certification as requested by the Managing Director and he was not given the option of time limitation to pass the ICAN certification that would have been an ideal situation to be grandfathered for the position in a civilized society.

Instead, he was redeployed to the Ministry of Commerce and Industries as a Civil Service Accountant without any clear cut job schedule to keep him out of the loop, no leave bonus, no relocation allowance from Ijebu Ode to Abeokuta, he was treated like a vomit by the system, that was the way the Managing Director understood the policy of *"take care of the Accountant"*

A few weeks after redeployment, the Accountant was attacked by armed robbers and almost died. He was left with a limping lower extremity. People would point accusing fingers in his direction of his past ordeal, but like the Oracle wrote in the past, Ogun State people enjoyed silent wars and sometimes voodoo attacks. In the case of the Accountant and the Management of the company both methods were assumed.

Despite the fact that this writer was never on the right note with the Accountant I had compassion for him. From the little time we worked together I knew how loyal he was to the management or Dr Olubajo except he carried it too far.

Each time the Accountant was with the General Manager, he would hang a stupid fixed smile on his face like a dog waiting for a bone or crumbs from the master's table. I could not stand either of them, however, to keep my sanity, I kept my distance from them someone might call it eye service, but to me, it was the lowest level of degradation of human behavior.

What went wrong?

"He who stands for nothing will fall for anything."

— Alexander Hamilton

Imaginable

The company had a confidential Secretary. She was a very beautiful black lady, about 5ft.9in tall who became the subject of problems between the General Manager and the Accountant. She had mesmerizing eyes, tempting rolling pelvic hips, covetous lips and the eyes of Jezebel.

Both of them desired her, but she tactically rebuffed them. I can recall one of my friends also wanted her like every other man in the City. She attracted men in the City of Abeokuta like honey to bees. Whatever it was in her, everyman wanted a taste of her like Hennessey liquor drink particularly those with money and power.

As fate would have it, she was attracted to an aspiring manager. A young man named John from another government agency within the vicinity of our company's temporary location. John was a very good looking guy, about 5.11 tall. Clean shaved with a penciled mustache, he looked like a guy who visited the gym, a guy like him in the western world would be in the cover page of GQ magazine, and he had only one human error, he smokes cigarettes a lot when he gets upset.

The relationship of the Secretary with John irritated the General Manager and Accountant, and jointly, they formed a cartel against the innocent lady's choice. Her boyfriend was separated from his wife and had children. They both thought they could start a new life together.

The entirely whole company staff went to the traditional wedding in a nearby City in a very charged and stimulated atmosphere because something unimaginable had happened. What was it?

She was already five months pregnant. The marriage was a cover-up because the family of the first wife put pressure on the young man. Some rumored, he was threatened with voodoo. Whatever it was, and he ended up with two wives.

The pride and joy of the Secretary was deflated. At work, she became the subject of ridicule between the Accountant and the General Manager. Shamefully, one could hear them openly making fun of her, as if she wasn't even there.

"Boss me, aah! Oga o," Peter the Accountant would say as soon as he passed by the confidential Secretary's office on his way to the General Manager's office.

"Ah aha! Under my nose here!" Anthony, the General Manager replied mischievously.

"What a strange and wonderful world" Peter said with a very funny mockery ascent of Ijebu dialect.

"Boss me, you are an experienced man. Can you explain to me sir how a man can manage two women under the same roof? I want to share from your wealth of wisdom sir?" he said.

"I don't have that kind of experience," Anthony replied with a stupid smile on his thin lips.

"Boss me, you have experience and at least you have friends with two to three wives," he asked mischievously.

"I told you I don't have such experiences. What is your problem?" he said with a smile that exposed his tiny set of teeth.

The General Manager had a funny way of laughing his two shoulder blades were jerking up and down like former President George Bush of the United States of America.

He knew what was coming next as he pointed to the chair for him to sit down. It was time to gossip again.

"But, how can a man ask for sex from two women in the same house?" Peter asked as he sat down directly opposite the General Manager with a hanging stupid smile on his face.

"Well, you just divide the sleep nights between the two women on an every other week basis." Anthony replied with a straight face.

"Do you think all the women and the husband have a round table conference on this division of labor?" he joked.

"Which schedule are you talking about?" He jokingly asked

"You know what I mean sir" He said.

"No, the husband does his sex job schedule all alone, and he will just give it to the women, they sleep with him on every other week arrangement" he replied.

"Aah haa Aah, suppose one of the women was having her monthly period what will happen to the every other week arrangement?" Peter inquired further.

Like a two year old kid as each answer led to another question which was the reason for calling them the terrible two in those days by the staff of the company.

"That is when problem comes into the arrangement," he said.

"But how?" Peter asked.

"In some cases, most of them will have a weekly arrangement and the woman sleeping with the husband will be the one cooking for the family, and all the children eat from the same source to avoid food poison," he said.

"I see, in case of food poison, she can kill her own children also" Peter said with a smile on his face showing his missing front tooth.

Anthony would sometimes give graphic details in a very loud voice for the Secretary to hear the conversation.

"I see, but boss do you think your Secretary is enjoying the every night or weekly arrangement?" Peter asked.

"You should be asking her not me," Anthony said.

"I can't believe that none of us could sleep with the lady. The way she rolls her butt every now and then and that stupid smoker has her every night." He said with regret.

"Boss me, what are the reasons, beyond lust or stupidity for a man to have more than a woman in the house. I can't even manage the one I have," he asked.

"That is where you're wrong. Our fathers have good reasons for this part of our culture, as soon as the children are old enough both the wife and children always neglected the feelings of the head of the family, as a result of this, the man takes on the second wife," he explained.

"Is that the only reason or one of the reasons?" Peter questioned.

"Well, there are other reasons. The first wife may not be nice to the husband's family, and with the support of the family, the man would be encouraged to get another woman. Or if the woman was unable to have a child, instead of divorce or adoption that are alien to African culture, most likely option would be marriage to the second or third wife. Others could base their reason on religion. He said.

The Accountant was silent for a brief period of time before his next question.

What about educated Muslims? He asked.

"Well Muslims are allowed by the Koran to marry as many as four wives if they can afford it. Our custom places no limitation on the number of wives you can have if you have the resources" He explained further.

"I see" Peter said.

"I could see why Fela Anikulapo Kuti married 27 wives in one day because of tradition" the Accountant added.

"No leave Fela out of this discussion. He did it to escape the child molestation and abduction case brought against him by the Federal Military government of that time" he corrected.

The worst scenario of everything was visible to all. Her husband John's office was in the next building and in most instances he would come out of his office to smoke cigarettes.

Peter would peep out of his office which was almost adjacent to that of John, and immediately would rush to the General Manager's office and to begin their conversation about

Marie and her husband. The way they went about it one would think they were having a management meeting.

It was shameful.

"Boss me, can you see the boy? He is smoking again. He is going to die very soon of lung cancer," Peter said.

"That is his third cigarette in two hours," Anthony said.

"Boss me; I did not know you were counting the cigarettes. Look at how the smoke is coming out of his mouth and nose at the same time like a locomotive engine," he said.

"Maybe the women did not sleep with him last night, or one of them gave him too much sex, he looks tired and worried," Anthony said.

"I wonder who slept with him last night. Do you think Marie did?" Peter said in a loud enough voice for the Secretary to hear the conversation.

"Do you want to ask her?" Anthony said mischievously.

Marie could not take it anymore. She started crying loudly and when she got home she gave a detailed account of the mental torture at work to her husband. He came to my office the next day and wanted to file a complaint on the matter to the General Manager.

The stress of managing the two women in addition to the work was probably too much for John. He exchanged pleasantries with me. He needed a friend that would understand his emotional stress to confide in.

Most of the time he visited his wife at work he would stop by my office and we would talk for couple of minutes. He found me to be very sincere and started confiding in me. That particular afternoon he expressed to me the problem his wife was having at work with the Accountant.

Peter, the Accountant had gone out for lunch one afternoon where he met Marie at a local restaurant. They exchanged pleasantries and he asked how and when the Secretary shared intimacy nights with her husband.

"How do you guys work things out?" he asked mischievously.

"What things, sir?" she said.

"I mean sleep, I heard yours was a weekly arrangement," he said, with that same stupid smile on his face.

"What weekly arrangement?" she said, she pretended to be ignorant of the question.

"Sex or do you guys do three-somes like in the pornographic movies?" he asked as if it was a genuine question.

"That is my private life," she said firmly.

"There is no privacy here when the other woman is involved. Let me advise you young lady, the future for you is very bright but not with that "smoking Joe" you call your husband. Just drop his baby for him and come with me, I will take good care of you better than that struggling idiot," he said.

That was when she decided to tell her husband about the mental torture she was going through at work. She was detailed about the Accountant not the General Managers' involvement and that was why her husband came to see me one afternoon before he had a meeting with the boss.

"I don't think that would be the right thing to do my friend," I said in response to his story.

"Show I have to besides the General Manager is from the same home town as me he'll understand," he said. Show was his pet way of addressing me.

"John, if I were you, I would look for another job for my wife in another agency. Whatever it is, do not discuss the situation with the boss" I said without details.

He ignored my advice and went straight to the General Manager.

"Good afternoon sir," he said.

Anthony looked at him with a thin smile on his face; he ignored John's extended hand for a handshake, he just directed him to the seat.

"How are you doing?" he said.

"I am doing fine sir" John replied.

"You should be" he said with a laugh that covered what he did not say out loud which was, how John will not be doing well- sleeping with two women under the same roof.

"I have a problem with Peter your Accountant sir. He's constantly mocking and harassing my wife at work. I would like you, to order him to leave my wife alone" he said, after giving a detailed account of what happened on various occasions.

Anthony listened to everything but what he said was not what John was expecting as he stormed out of his office and came to relate everything to me.

"You told me not to go," he said. He was fuming with anger. He probably needed a cigarette to smoke by now as his right hand was shaking.

"But you went!" I said.

"You know more than you told me, don't you?" he asked.

"And what happened?" I said ignoring his Statement.

"Can you believe what that "bastard" said after I told him my concern about the Accountant," he said.

"Calm down," I said.

"I felt like shooting him," he said.

"John, you don't have a gun, you were just mad at him. Tell me what happened," I said.

"After I finished talking to him he told me he was not a marriage counselor. His job was to manage a business, not to manage the sex life of a young man with a "dangling dick" and if I do not have anything serious to say, I should leave his office." He said

"You must be kidding" I said.

"Besides that, the Accountant walked in and both of them were laughing at me" he added.

"Now you see why I told you not to go and if you must know, both of them wanted to sleep with your wife before you married her," I revealed to him.

That was how close the Accountant and the General Manager were to each other, before the crises.

Throughout the time of Governor Osoba, the Accountant disappeared from circulation and the Managing Director had a free hand with the project. He lacked direction, but he was still protected by the system of manipulation and frustration of the biggest project in the State, probably in Africa's pharmaceutical industry.

The Management of the company turned out to be a one man show, for a man who never had any industrial exposure or knew what to do or what plan to fast track the project.

However, attempts were made to sell the project off to Bayer Pharmaceuticals and other pharmaceutical companies from Lagos, only if the buyer would have an Ijebu man or woman as management that was always the hidden condition.

Bayer and Pfizer Pharmaceutical Companies in Lagos made an attempt to buy or manage the project and they had only people from Egba and Awori in their top management team. The government wouldn't play ball and everyone knew the reason for the refusal of all the proposals of the bidders.

Eventually, because of politics and manipulations, the project remained abandoned. The Accountant was recuperating from the attack in an unknown location and Colonel Akintonde became the new military administrator of the State.

What did he do?

"If A is a success in life, then A equals x plus y plus z. Work is x; y is play; and z is keeping your mouth shut"

- Albert Einstein

9

THE RIPPLES OF HOPE

The knew administrator Col Daniel Akintonde from the State of Ogun was a close associate of my childhood friend late Colonel Olu Akiode of the Military Intelligence on Child Avenue Apapa Lagos. Col. Olu Akiode was assigned to work with Major General Olanrewaju as his Military Assistant in the Federal Ministry of Communication. We grew up together in Ekotedo Ibadan and attended Nigeria Defense Academy Kaduna in the early seventies.

Col. Akintonde was a different person as soon as he became the administrator. He wanted to investigate the disappearance of the Federal grant of 40 million naira to the Gateway Pharmaceutical Company after he read the new petition from the Accountant.

However, the Administrator of the State did not do his homework properly before he announced on State owned radio and television that he was going to set up an Administrative Board of Inquiry.

A five man committee to investigate the missing money, with the secretary from Ministry of Commerce and Chairman a former Chief Accountant Agric. Development corporation, also a staff person from the Ministry of Justice and Ministry of Health, and contributions were invited from the public.

The Administrative Board of inquiry read my past contributions that were on file, including the plan of action note I wrote in my resignation letter five years earlier. When the details became public and the names of the military big guys were mentioned the Administrator just like the past civilian Governor Osoba, chickened out and the report of the panel never saw the light of day until now.

The only positive thing that came out of the inquiry was the removal of the Managing Director. He was given the same treatment he gave his Accountant. He was also redeployed to the State Ministry of Commerce and Industry and the Accountant was redeployed to his old job at the company.

However, the former Managing Director was retired and an unconfirmed source said it was because he was sleeping on duty in the State Ministry of Commerce.

Six months later, like I predicted in the plan of actions management used, the company rolled out its first pharmaceutical product "GATEMOL" and at the time Colonel Akintode was Administrator for the State of Ogun.

That meant the project's takeoff plans passed consecutively through Governors Onabanjo, Diya, Popoola, Raji Rasaki, Lawal, Joseph, Osoba and Akintode before the people of the State saw the reality of the intention conceived in 1982.

However, Gov. Gbenga Daniel sold the project as almost a giveaway concession like he did with most projects in the State Governor Ibikunle Amosun would be kind enough to review.

Furthermore, Col. Akintode would not budge when the Oracle visited him in his office on the need to our company's products for the new Ogun State Stadium and New world Paint from Drucker Industries Limited at Sango Ota in the State.

We were doing fine. We recruited from Berger paints and IPWA in Lagos and our products could be found in most of the stores in Lagos, Onitsha, Ariara Market, Itagarawu in Lagos, Labaowo in Ibadan and the Arakale market in Akure. We just wanted to do good business with Ogun State Government.

The Governor told us, there was no plan to paint Ogun State Stadium although he knew my relationship with Col. Olu Akiode. His military colleagues and I believed him, or why would he be untruthful to us since our contact with him was his military colleague?

Surprisingly, I was having a drink with Mr. Bankole at Abeokuta Club one night, when he told me, his company Premier Paint was literarily awarded a contract to supply paint to the same stadium the Governor told us it was not going to be painted.

Such was the system in Nigeria business; as soon as you submitted a proposal for any project it would be rejected and be given to another company.

As a result of the above, I never attempted to seek any government contract. It was pointless, particularly if they knew your reputation as someone who would not over invoice, or cook a document.

"I will not serve that in which I no longer believe, whether it calls itself my home, my fatherland, or my church: and I will try to express myself in some mode of life or art as freely as I can and as wholly as I can, using for my defense the only arms I allow myself to use -- silence, exile, and cunning."

— James Joyce, a Portrait of the Artist as a Young Man

10

THE TASKS AHEAD

GPC was not the only project in the State of Ogun in all those years. But it was a perfect example on how projects were conceived and managed in the State, however, there were other successful projects with strong internal problem, like the Ogun Property and

Investment Corporation, OPIC, Tower Gate Insurance, Gateway banks, Lapeleke Gateway Bricks and others but they were plagued with problems between the Egba and Ijebu. It must be noted that only the projects with corporate offices in Abeokuta and Lagos succeeded and can still be seen today.

In the State Ministry of Commerce and Industries many projects were buried or never saw the light of the day because of their political locations. The glass factory in Owode Local government and any future new Governor of the State would have to dig into all the buried files in the State.

What happened next? After Col. Akintonde left the State and another Governor Group Captain Sam Ewang came, he sacked many people because they were believed to be members of secret societies in the State.

Nevertheless, by 1996 the Oracle had left the country. When Gov. Segun Osoba returned as Action AD or Congress Party Governor of the State, based on a new report, he continued his "Aremo" chieftaincy title acquisition of every town mentality and he never learned anything.

He did not perform as a good Governor as expected by the Egba and it was very easy for the People's Democratic Party (PDP) through General Olusegun Obasanjo the President of Nigeria to get him out of office.

Then, one of the smartest politicians and mostly misunderstood manipulator with lots of political intrigues became the new State Governor for the next eight years of nightmares in the State of Ogun. Both the Egba and the Ijebu could not understand because he was from the minority Remo side of the State.

Why did Governor Osoba lose his re-election bid to Governor Gbenga Daniel?

The second coming of Aremo Osoba as the Governor of the State was indeed a nightmare for the Egba and Egbado now called Yewa because the Governor was busy running for a second term from his first day in office and acquired more local titles rather than facing the real job of governance for the State and the people.

Any serious observer would note that the architectural views of towns in Egba, Egbado now called Yewa and Awori apart from Ota and Abeokuta in proximity to modernized Lagos State looked like 18th Century societies. They were more like glorified villages begging for development.

Governor Osoba was a blind man to civilization just like President Obasanjo was. Both of them did not see improvement in their community as part of the deal.

In other words, they were in government for personal reasons. They never constructed modern roads for dual carriage for the State capital. It was still the same way Governor Popoola left the State several years before.

They could not understand the need to transform a society or roads to dual carriages or overhead bridges. They enjoyed their people living like villagers instead of learning from what makes the Ijebu a better community than the Egba in terms of rural development. The development in the State of Lagos did not rub off on them.

The foresights and recognition of a better structure in Ijebu Province must not be taken away from them. This is the area the Egba must learn to work on. It is a bitter truth that must be recognized as to why past Egba leadership failed.

An average Egba or Ijebu man would wonder, if Ijebu had half of the Federal political opportunities the Egba had in the past decades with a two time presidency and a military Head of State, what would be the effect of it on the Ijebu Community.

Governor Segun Osoba's performance or lack of it created room for the removal of the AD control party and their ritual gatherings of the Afenifere group at Ijebu Igbo under the leadership of Papa Adesanya and increasing need to move away from the past of the so-called Awolowo faithful. When in actual facts, the people could not reflect or reconcile the performance of the AD Governors with that of Awolowo in the past.

All these, along with other factors of second or third term ambition of "Aremo of every City" in the State created the opening for the switch to PDP. Even if the election was rigged, it was anticipated because of the failed leadership of Governor Osoba. His style and performance opened the door for PDP to win Ogun State's Governorship election.

According to the news report by Papa Adewolu who was a classmate of General Olusegun Obasanjo in the High School, who said in an interview that it was Governor Ibikunle Amosun who succeeded Governor Daniel that introduced Gbenga Daniel to Ogun State's powerful man, General Obasanjo who was the former President of Nigeria. Do we have any reason to doubt Papa Adewolu?

Subsequent events led Senator Amosun to join another political party ANPP. Under which he ran for Governorship against the man he brought to the State from nowhere. He lost or never really got the true result of the election as every effort to investigate the fraud as alleged was muddled with legal adjournments until Gov. Daniel completed his term of four years, The people of the State never knew the true result of the election.

Otunba Daniel was a business man from Lagos and the United Kingdom. He spent his early childhood in the City of Ibadan between Oke Ado, Oke Bola and NTC Road. His liquid assets could not be established. Some described him as a struggling businessman before he became the Governor and the information about his assets declaration was exaggerated or anticipated in lieu of future aggrandizement.

Assets in Nigeria could be not tied to any social security number like in the United States, the United Kingdom and other developed societies, which anyone can verify online. All you need to do is search by county, State or region even by names and all the investments associated with any name would be revealed.

Whatever you wrote in those days became prima facie and the system of Nigeria's asset declaration was faulty. The system accepted any property mentioned on paper as an asset without official verification. It was sad!

Just like Dr. Alex Ekweme, the Vice President to President Sheu Shagari between 1979 to 1983. He had less than all he declared when the government was probed by military government of General Buhari in 1984.

Governor Daniel at the end of his first term in office (and at the time when late president Yar'Adua declared N850 million in assets) declared N4.5 billion in assets and the State of Ogun was never comfortable with him again, it was either out of envy or the source of the wealth or assets were questionable.

The Ogun State House of Assembly members were terrorized. Some had armed-attackers visit them at home as reported in most of the online news media. There were unconfirmed rumors that Governor Daniel had killer groups working for him. They said most of the murders in the State were organized by the Governor.

Could they be right?

Years later, in a court case he had with the EFCC he was specifically warned by the Court on the safety of witnesses to confirm this assumption, before and after the death of High Chief

Olumide the government star witness in a strange and suspicious way on the Gulf Course owned by the High Chief of Egba.

Most of the contacts to government records, which could be used to find out all the money assumed missing were blocked, and those asking questions were mysteriously killed in some form of strange deaths the press reported. Some were fired from work, whatever it was became a concern to all the people in the State. His political rival in the State Dipo Dina a brother in-law to my childhood friend former naval officer Dr. Oloruntoba Elegbe was killed.

However, from a Governor that started well, but became a nuisance during his second term. The second term victory against Senator Ibikunle Amosun was contested in Appeal Court but the case was never allowed to come up for hearing due to many legal bottle necks and after lots of adjournments, the public and the petitioner lost interest in the case, that was the system of judiciary administration in Nigeria, many sensational cases were lost to the system.

Governor Daniel was however, smarter than former Gov. Osoba, he established a funny looking cargo Airport between Ilishan and Ishara in the Remo area of the State, and had the 30 miles road between Abeokuta and Sagamu lined with street or road lights.

Apart from the one mile road construction between Ibara and Oke Ilewo in the State Capital, nothing concrete or significant could be pointed to what the smiling Governor did for his people REMO or other members of the State.

It was a case of Abracadabra, the more you see, the less you know. The street or roads lights instead of opening the eyes of the people, Infact diverted their eyes from seeing how Governor Daniel was managing the State.

It was so sad to see the innocent people of Ogun State of the two provinces (Ijebu and Egba) in the darkness of ideas in the 21st Century, in a government like that of Gbenga Daniel without respect for other two tiers of government

Governor Daniel almost dissolved the State Assembly for questioning his style of leadership. He saw the Governorship more like a military administrator. It was on record that under Gbenga Daniel, 9 was a majority instead of 15 in the State House of Assembly of 24 members, because he had different agenda for 100 billion naira fund and he was planning to use the State Assembly to rubber stamp the approval for his government with unclear and untitled projects.

When in actuality, most of the developments in the fund were meant for his people Remo, Ijebu no matter his good intention his refusal to place all facts on the table made him a suspect more than the true intentions of the fund.

Governor Daniel just like Governor Bisi Onabanjo did in the eighties at one time threatened to remove the new Alake of Egbaland Oba Adedotun Gbadebo over issues that affected the distribution of amenities in the State.

The government could not account for the State money from all properties allegedly sold in Lagos and it could not be ascertained if the legal action on the matter was resolved on not as the case was adjourned like many other cases involving corruption and abuse of office in the country.

Among various allegations against the Governor were that the Local governments became donors to the Governor's personal and political fund rather than to their communities, and those expected to take action on the anti-democratic behavior of the Governor, turned their eyes other way including former President

Obasanjo, the President of Nigeria Dr. Jonathan and late President Yar'Adua.

The rational for lack of action or inactions on the part of these men could not be justified. No reasonable person could explain it either, maybe they needed the Governor to keep the State with the PDP in future elections; which was a plan that eventually failed because Asiwaju Tinubu the leader of Action Congress of Nigeria ACN and former Gov. Olusegun Osoba closed ranks, the unity between the two led to the removal of the political infrastructure of Governor Gbenga Daniel, however, his government left the State with 57 billion naira debts, maybe the structural removal saved the government.

Will Ogun State improve under Governor Amosun, a former student of Ogun State Polytechnics, only time will tell?

Whatever the strengths and weaknesses of Governor Daniel in all these must be examined in the future for checks and balances in the State political structure, a system that allows any Governor to dip his hands in the people's fund without any control. Or to engineer the close down of the State Assembly and spend money or sell the State resources without approval are some of the flaws in the 1999 constitution.

Maybe the removal of immunity clause will be the solution and adequate understanding and usage of the Freedom of Information (FOI) Law will help to overcome those ugly behaviors of elected leaders. Again time will tell.

The above were some of the burdens and problems in most of the States in Nigeria and it was the same reason most Nigerians left the country and still leaving because nothing has changed.

Those in exile carried the burden of these economic stress and uncertainty of political relevance even as immigrants they never stopped wondering if the system would change.

Whenever those who stole from the system were charged to court by the police or the compromised EFCC, they were released on bail and the case would be adjourned continually till it was forgotten. The society lost hope in the future for everything and blamed the military for an unfinished revolution.

The people of Ogun State, indeed all Nigerians blamed the military for the faulty constitution left behind that continue to protect the elected officials rights to steal with the immunity clause which some of us vowed to remove one day. Nigerians particularly the youths all continue to lament like the Jewish nation at the bank of river Babylon.

Even those at home never stopped wondering what happened to the democracy they all fought to snatch away from the military. What about the sacrifices made by all in the June 12th 1993 elections and the struggle since 1960? All these things made this writer to become a columnist for an online news media companies. I wrote about the establishment of a State and City police system for the country, the need to establish a Mayoral System of administration for all our cities; and an hourly payment system and removal of the immunity clause.

We sent direct emails and letters to various agencies and in most cases the system ignored everything and the immigrants continued to wonder if those in government in Nigeria were sane people. We wondered why on earth anyone would steal from his country with the active participation of a powerless judiciary.

Maybe one day, a Savior will come and the society will be freed. Maybe the Savior will not be treated like Jesus was, or if HE or SHE would be recognized.

We were exporting a new type of democracy through writing and just like my friend said, writers like you don't die they live two hundred years more on each book you write.

The journey remains tougher than planned, for most of us the best thing is to recognize the need to adjust to the reality of the new world and environment, some did not.

Like the oracle, we saw our future and decided to go for it in America, in Europe and in all the nations on Earth. While we still hope and pray for the people at home, if home is indeed the best place for any human being, it is also where you find rest and peace of mind, the safety of your family, the comfort of your spiritual being and where your dreams and goals are achievable, home is no longer where your parents were born. Home may Infact be your journey.

77

The Day Sola Died

1980 Student Union elections had been won and lost, just as we settled down to the type of leadership the new Student Union President Wassiu Popoola was going to foist on the new institution, the previous leadership was too brief to make any impact and Wassiu Popoola was going to be the proper foundation for Ogun State Polytechnic Student Unionism.

The Business Administration department was very bitter and disorganized for the loss of the presidency to the Accountancy Department, because of the internal rivalry between Sola Alakija and Kehinde Sokeye and by the time Kehinde emerged as the candidate, we knew Popoola would be too difficult to beat and Sola Alakija was persuaded by the Popoola group to run for the office of welfare which he won and Kehinde Sokeye was out of the loop, this writer was a prominent member of the school editorial Board was ready to assist the Union with the welfare programs.

Sola Alakija was the son of a prominent politician of the first Republic Dr Alakija, his father's connection was an inspiration to him and his political career was almost assured by President Sheu Shagari a long term friend of his father in the Prime Minister Tafawa Balewa government in the sixties, if he could have at least a degree from the University or Polytechnic from all the information and correspondence he exposed to me.

When he lost the primary for the Union presidency, it became a temporary setback for him and his new position as Welfare Secretary was his determination to make an impact to help his career.

He asked the school authority to purchase the first Ambulance for Clinic on the Onikolobo Campus, a decision that was approved. He asked for the expansion of the cafeteria from the two room utility section on the campus, it was approved, he asked for many issues that improved the life styles on the campus this Oracle Zents Kunle Sowunmi was his trusted friend and adviser, somehow Kehinde Sokeye who lost the presidency was also my friend, but he never stopped calling me "Zik of Poly" which eventually became my political name on the campus, because I was able to balance the relationship between the student Union controlled by the Accountancy Department with those of the aggrieved members of the Business Department due to the bitter politics on how Kehinde Sokeye won the primary in the Department but lost the general election.

However, Kehinde had constituted himself to be leader of the Opposition to the new and young student Union, as a member of the editorial Board most of the stories to disorganize the Union were discouraged and we knew we had to bring in Sokeye's group into the business of the union if we have to make any impact and how would that be?

The opportunity for it finally came when the National Association of Ogun State was formed and we had to nominate a candidate for the Presidency of the association. Sola Alakija was routing for me to run for it since Popoola was not interested, but I felt Kehinde would be a better candidate for the position, I was asked to either run for the office or find a candidate for it. I had to meet with Kehinde Sokeye on it if he would take it.

After laying down all the benefits of the duties of a national President of Ogun State Students Association, he asked me why I was not interested; I told him he could do it better, and my job will be to coordinate the political end of his winning by getting the guys from University of Lagos, Ibadan and Ife not to show interest on the job because of my years of association with "Laadoo" Ladele President of Student Union of Yaba Tech Lagos , on one condition he would stay off the back of Wassiu Popoola's government, he agreed with the it. He became the President of Ogun State Student Association and University of Lagos nominated the General Secretary.

Kehinde Sokeye primary job was to coordinate with the State Government on Bursary Award and other issues, he needed three other people to work with him in addition to the five members of his executive, Kehinde asked me to help, and I did. We met regularly with Governor Bisi Onabanjo on the Bursary and my contact with Chief Sesan Soluade the Deputy Governor was good enough for our goal, the deputy Governor was my High School French and Literature teacher in days at Lisabi Grammar School. I was able to get the mood of the Governor from him until Governor Bisi Onabanjo refused to pay the Bursary and we had to chase him out of his office. It became a legal issue which we won against the government.

In between these we were preparing for the examination and Cost Accounting was a bit of problem for Sola and we agreed to brain storm later in the evening after an overnight study. He was to meet with me by 6 pm, he never showed up.

In those days, no telephone, no, email, no texting, we just expected the person to show up. And he never did. I went to bed and he appeared to me in my dreams, he was standing outside the examination hall, I asked him to come in for the test he refused, he said he had all the answers in the folder he had with him, and he walked away from the text center, when I woke up, I did not think of it until I got to his house early in the morning to finish with the review when I heard he died by 3.15 pm the previous day through intracranial hemorrhage. It was then, I figured out the meaning of his appearance to me in the dream, he came to say goodbye to his friend.

His death affected everyone on the Campus and the whole of Abeokuta was touched with his death, we knew he lost his brother 40 days earlier to his death and he was probably depressed but the day he died was June 24, 1980, it was his birthday, the examination was cancelled for a week, it was the first death on the Campus, we had no experience on how to handle such a tragedy, besides, it was the death a leader who cared for the students, and we all cried as Sola was carried with the Ambulance he made the authority to purchase, it was like he knew his journey would be over on the campus.

The night before he was buried, he appeared again to me in my dream with a red soaked Band-Aid on his forehead, he said he was not dead, he wanted me to feel the soaked blood on his head, I could not, but as we carried his corpse, I was wondering if he was just in a coma when he was pronounced dead, and if he was indeed back to life inside the casket.

Sola was buried somewhere in Onikolobo Abeokuta very close to the school he loved and gave his best. His death killed my interest in politics and it was a surprise to many of my friends somehow I felt I could do something in his memory and dedicating few pages of this book to his memories would be one of them. Forty days after Sola died, his baby brother also died in a mysterious way.

It meant within 120 days his mother lost three sons what a tragedy, Mrs. Alakija died about two years ago from the information

I got from our common friend Hon. Igbore Sofolahan from Lagos State. May her soul and those of her children and my friend in particular rest in peace.

In 1996 in my little comfort in Dallas Texas in the United States of America, I received a phone call from Kehinde Akinbode on the death of the friend who called me "Zik of Poly" it was sad to hear the death of Kehinde Sokeye, a good friend, very humorous, one could never imagine him without a smile on his face, and every day we argued and still found peace with each other.

I have never stopped thinking how and why a political star as eloquent as Kehinde Sokeye could die at a time his State needed him and I still remember how we made him to sit on the Governor's chair in 1980 for 15-30 minutes when we chased Ayekooto Gov. Bisi Onabanjo out when he refused to pay the Bursary award , and how Kehinde defended the Ogun State students Association in court like a trained lawyer, and his funny tie which I joked with, the pin pong table tennis in front of his house at Ijeja Abeokuta which we played and his house which was the gathering place for politics. Just like Harold Robin said in one of his books, some events of life can have your memories. He had mine. I missed my Buddy.

12

BETTER DAYS AHEAD

In 1996, I stood on the street of West End in Dallas Texas, in the United States of America, on the ground was an inscription that the City of Dallas was established in 1847, seventeen years after Abeokuta became the harbor for the Egba, and I never stopped wondering what kept us behind, after reading all the chapters of this book the question in mind of the readers is what do we do next?

Let us look into the future of this great State with hope and expect success from Governor Ibikunle Amosun, a pioneer student of Ogun State Polytechnics with the hope the State or the people that first saw civilization in Nigeria with contributions from Thomas Birch Freeman, Rev. Henry Townsend among others will be first among equals in the country again.

The mistake of 1948 must never be repeated like the loss of the University due to flimsy politics, or that of the misplaced priority in Western State in 1972 when one the sons of this State was governor. It is also the believe of this writer, at the end of the second term in office of Governor Ibikunle Amosun overhead bridges will be in Odopotu, Odo Shenbora, Ilara, Ilaro, Otta Akaka, Sagamu, Obantoko, Wasimi, Owode, Shiun, Orile Ilugun, Obada Oko and Ogun River will have dual carriage roads on both sides which is similar to what is done in civilized societies.

It is more than just a dream; it can be the beginning of hope for our children and generation unborn. It is possible just like former President of the United State of America President Williams Jefferson Clinton said, "We can use everything that is right in us to correct whatever is wrong in us".

We the people of the old Abeokuta and Ijebu provinces in the State of Ogun must use everything that is good in us to improve the State, we must learn from each other and leave behind a legacy of trust and commitment to the future of our people, the primitive war files of Kiriji that was the foundation of our problems must be kept permanently in the achieves or museums.

Perhaps it will interest readers in 1914 Abeokuta had the first electriCity in the Yoruba land, some said it was even the first in Nigeria, in 2013 we have the first overhead bridge from the government of Governor Ibikunle Amosun, it means 99 years is how far the progress of Abeokuta and Egba community was kept behind civilization.

We can fast track development in the State and we must cooperate with Lagos State just like the State of New Jersey does with State of New York, or the cities that are within two States like Kansas City is crammed in between States of Kansas and Missouri, the cooperation here can be seen from rail transportation, water supplies and energy, this should be our goals for the some of our cities sharing borders with Lagos State.

Let us ask for Mayoral system of government for our cities all over the State and the establishment of State and City police to improve on the security of our people, we can do this if we seek constitutional amendment in this respect, this is how the policy of manipulation can be turned to policy of even development.

If the Ijebu must have a State, the government must send a bill to the House of Assembly to adopt the request which can be forwarded to the Federal Authority, but the Oracle will advise on the need to discourage a fruitless exercise as State creation will be a difficult task than the implementation of Mayoral System of Administration which will fast track development to all the cities of the State.

Winning is the name of the game, let us win this State for our children and generations to come. Let us not really only on the glory of the past, from Oduduwa to Lisabi or that of Obafemi Awolowo and those who gave us the hope to believe in ourselves, It is now for us to give hope to the coming generation through our services that must see everyone in the State as a member of the same family, not as Ijebu, Egba, Awori, Yewa, Egun but as Ogun State, this entity can still be number one again if we start now.

May God bless the people of Ogun State and Nigeria.

INDEX

Abeokuta Club: A social Mother Club to seniors in Egba lands

Abeokuta Elites: A social Club in Abeokuta

Abeokuta: The Capital of Ogun State Nigeria. The tradition home of the Egba

Abeti Aja: Traditional Yoruba Cap

Abiola, MKO: Winner of annulled 1993 presidential election in Nigeria.

Abuja: The Federal Capital of Nigeria since 1990

Adenekan Yomi: Engineer and director of works in Ogun State

Agbada: Big tradition full regalia dress

Agbongbo Akala: The title given to Lisabi by his people, the Egba

Agemo: The outcome of Alagemo more like masquerade

AGGS: Abeokuta Girls Grammar School

AGS: Abeokuta Grammar School

Ajoke Mohammed: Wife of late Head of State of Nigeria

Akarigbo: The traditional title for the King of Remo in Ogun State

Akintode Col: A military Administrator of Ogun State in Nigeria

Alaafin: The traditional title of Oyo King from Old Oyo Empire

Alaafin: The Traditional title of the King of Oyo

Alaaren: A traditional way to greet the Ijebu people

Alagemo: Traditional Ijebu fetish club

Alake: The paramount ruler of Egbaland

Amosun, Ibikunle, the Governor of Ogun State from 2011.

Angola: A country in Central Africa, very rich in crude oil

ArticleBased.com: A news blog for articles

Aselite: Abeokuta Social Elite Club

Asero: Area within Abeokuta City

Awolowo, Obafemi: Leader of Yoruba race

Awori: A sub ethnic group in Ogun State very closes to Lagos

Awujale: The paramount ruler of Ijebuland

Balogun, Ayodele Col.: The first Military Governor of Ogun State in Nigeria in 1976

BBHS: Baptist Boys High School Abeokuta

CBN: Central Bank of Nigeria

Cooper& Lybrand: An Accounting Firm in Lagos

EFCC: Nigeria equivalence of FBI

Egba: The people of Abeokuta and its surrounding villages and towns

Egbado now called Yewa: A sub ethnic group in Ogun State part of old Abeokuta provinces now named after Yewa River.

Eghagha Col: The last military Governor of Ogun State before 1979

Egun: A sub ethnic group in Lagos and Ogun State

Gangan: Yoruba local talking Drums

GPC: Gateway Pharmaceutical Company Ijebu Ode

Hoover dam: A dam in Boulder County Nevada in the United States of America

Ibadan: The capital City of Old Western Region/State and Oyo State

Ijebu Ode: The City headquarters of the Ijebu people in Ogun State

Ijebu: The people of Ijebu towns

Ikere: The ear of Idowu comes naturally or can be implanted

Irukere: Made from Horse tail. A symbol of authority held by Yoruba Kings

Iya Ilu: The Big talking Drums

Juju: Voodoo assumed to have been discovered in Nigeria among the Yoruba

Kainji: HydroelectriCity dam across Niger River built in 1964 and commissioned in 1968

Kiriji: The internal Yoruba wars before the British colonization

Kpcpress.com: A news Blog of Korloki Publishing company

Kuto: An area within Abeokuta City

Lagos: Former Capital of Nigeria and Seat of government of Lagos State

LGS: Lisabi Grammar School Abeokuta

Lipede, Oyebade: The Alake of the Egbaland between 1972-2005.

Lisabi Elite: A social club in Abeokuta

Lisabi: The first known Hero of the Egba who freed them from Oyo Empire

Mohamed, Muritala: Nigeria Assassinated Head of State in 1976

Neto, Augustinho: First President of Angola

OAU: See Unife, Obafemi Awolowo University

Oba: Yoruba name for the King

Obantoko: An area within Abeokuta City

Obasanjo, General: Twice elected Nigeria President and Military Head of State

Obatala: The god of creation according to the Yoruba tribe in Africa

Ogun Poly: Ogun State Polytechnic now called MAPOLY

Ogun River: The source of this river is Kishi in the Kwara State

Ogun State: A State carved out of Western States in Nigeria in 1976

Ogun: The god of Iron usual worship by motor drivers and hunters among the Yoruba

Ojude Oba: A popular Ijebu festival

Olumo Rock

Ondo State: A State carved out of Western States in Nigeria in 1976

Opeke: A damsel or young lady

Oranmiyan: The last born of Oduduwa the progenitor of the Yoruba people

Oriaku: Igbo word for consumer of wealth

Orunmila: The god of divinity according to the Yoruba tribe in Africa

Oshun State: A State carved out of Oyo States in Nigeria in 1991

Owambe: Easy going and party loving group

Owode: A City in Owode Egba local government

Oyo Empire: Defunct Empire of the Yoruba people

Oyo State: A State carved out of Western States in Nigeria in 1976

Oyo: New Oyo town that emerged after the destruction of Old Oyo

Sagamu: The City headquarters of the Remo people in Ogun State also called Sagamu

Shekere: Percussion

Top Beer: Brand for a local beer in the Nigeria in the seventies

U.I: University of Ibadan established in 1948

Unife: University of Ife now Obafemi Awolowo University

Unilag: University of Lagos

Wahala: Yoruba word for problem

Whydah: The unverified source of the Ijebu by Awujale their paramount ruler

Yewa: Formerly called Egbado

Bibliography

Ajayi, Ade, & Smith, Robert 1964. PhD **Yoruba Warfare in the 19th Century** Cambridge Press

Arinze, Francis, PH.D. 1970. **Sacrifice in Ibo Religion** Ibadan University Press Nigeria

Boahen, Adu. Ph.D. 1965 **Topics in West African History Longman** Press United Kingdom

Okuwa, Bankole Ph.D. 2008 **"Political Unrest in Ogun State"** Nigeriaworld.com

Olabintan, Afolabi Ph.D. 1994 **"The graces, the grasses and the gains"** Nigeria

Sowunmi Zents MBA. 2011 "W**hat happened to our Democracy?**" Korloki Publishers NY USA

Sowunmi, Zents MBA. 2011" **Before the journey became Home**" Korloki Publishers NY USA

Sowunmi, Zents MBA. 2013 **"The Vultures and Vulnerable"** Korloki Publishers NY USA

GUARDING RULES

- Keep the smile on, it is good for the heart, besides it is free.
- Never allow the Devil to take your joy away.
- Learn to understand we operate in the world of Demons and Angels
- Give hope to the needy
- Encourage not discourage
- Find Humor in everything
- Learn to laugh at your own mistakes
- Keep going, if you stop you are done with.
- Don't take all your advice from failures you might be one yourself
- Stay focus on winning the battle of life.

Zents Kunle. Sowunmi is the President/CEO of the Allzents Groups Inc. a Business Consulting, Staffing/Training and Publishing Corporation with offices in Dallas Texas and Brooklyn New York. Zents Kunle Sowunmi was a staff of US Army Warrior Transition Battalion Fort Bliss Texas until February 2011.

He holds an MBA and several certifications. He is the author of *Before the Journey Became Home, President Obama: Hero or Villain of Capitalism? And "The Covenant Breakers", He* is also working on several other publications.

Zents Kunle Sowunmi books are available worldwide. For more information on the author or how to purchase autographed copies, please contact the author at zents@allzentstaff.com.

ALSO BY ZENTS KUNLE SOWUNMI

....

- ❖ President Obama: Hero or villain of Capitalism?
- ❖ Before the Journey Became Home
- ❖ 100 ways to Laugh
- ❖ Cien Maneras de Reir
- ❖ What happened to Our Democracy?
- ❖ Not a stranger Anymore
- ❖ The Covenant Breakers

Coming soon!!!

- ❖ The vultures and the Vulnerable
- ❖ The Loopholes
- ❖ The Price of Arab Revolution

Order copies of this author's books directly from **www.kpcbooks.com**

KORLOKI PUBLISHING COMPANY NEW YORK USA

www.ingramcontent.com/pod-product-compliance
Lightning Source LLC
Chambersburg PA
CBHW071307110426
42743CB00042B/1212